THE DREAM BOOK

The Modern Mystic's Guide to Dream Interpretation

RAPHAEL

Foreword by Dr. Michael Lennox

Published in the United States by St. Martin's Essentials,
an imprint of St. Martin's Publishing Group

 For information, address St. Martin's Publishing Group, 120 Broadway, New York, NY 10271.

www.stmartins.com

The Library of Congress Cataloging-in-Publication Data is available upon request.

ISBN 978-1-250-82875-0 (trade paperback)
ISBN 978-1-250-82876-7 (ebook)

Our books may be purchased in bulk for promotional, educational, or business use. Please contact your local bookseller or the Macmillan Corporate and Premium Sales Department at 1-800-221-7945, extension 5442, or by email at MacmillanSpecialMarkets@macmillan.com.

The Book of Dreams was first published in 1886
First St. Martin's Essentials Edition: 2022

10 9 8 7 6 5 4 3 2 1

CONTENTS

CONTENTS

PUBLISHER'S NOTE

Dreams are both completely commonplace and yet always otherworldly. Many of the experiences are universal: We've all woken up with the wisps of a dream floating in our minds only to forget it before we've had our morning coffee. We've all been warned not to bore others by recounting our midnight reveries (but what if it's a *really* good one?). And we've all found ourselves stiff with panic, heart racing in the grip of a nightmare. And yet each dream, whether bizarre or beautiful, is a unique creation of our own mind.

But do these dreams *mean* anything? Yes. No. Perhaps? In *The Dream Book* our mysterious author Raphael offers a guide to discerning the meanings of your dreams. The first section of the book is an easy-to-use dream dictionary. Simply look up the creatures and features you've dreamt of and you'll find the meaning associated with them. The second part of the book offers a more indirect method of dream interpretation using a system of ciphers based on intuition.

You may think this is simply a fun diversion or perhaps you are certain your dreams hold the key to the future. The choice is up to you. Sweet dreams!

FOREWORD

If you have picked up this fascinating little book, no doubt you are interested in dreams, and dream interpretation. We live in a modern world, at the beginning of a new century, and a new millennium. Our consideration of dreams and their value come out of the field of psychology, which by now is a mature science. Between what we understand about the unconscious, coupled with ever-growing knowledge of brain activity, we have come a long way since this book first appeared. When *The Book of Dreams* came out late in the nineteenth century, the Spiritualism movement was in its heyday, and there was tremendous interest in matters of the occult. No doubt, those who were captivated by mystical ideas responded powerfully to this book. It offers a systematic way of analyzing dreams, and then correlating what you find to symbolic meaning. It's something like a modern dream dictionary but without the perspective of what the field of psychology would eventually bring to this field. Its specific end game was predicting the future through dreams.

The year was 1886, a dynamic time of innovation and expansion. New York was becoming the center of the world. The Brooklyn Bridge was completed just a few years before, and the same year this book came out, the Statue of Liberty rose on the other side of New York Harbor. The Industrial Revolution had completely taken hold, and the amazing fortunes amassed at this time generated the moniker of the Gilded Age, and the divide between rich and poor began to truly segregate. Freud was fifteen years away from creating his seminal work that would utterly change the dreaming experience of human beings. Carl Jung, the father of modern dream work, was only eleven years old and still dreaming boyhood dreams.

To understand the environment that supported such a mystical publication, we have to back up a bit, about a century earlier. Indeed, the Industrial Revolution shifted the consciousness of the human race profoundly, as we earnestly moved away from country living and toward what would eventually become the modern world of manufacturing, world trade, and urban development. The broad sharing of ideas that came with the printing press and the expansion of education also allowed for explorations about humanity and spirituality to emerge in new ways. Out of cities rose the intellectual and cultural tropes that would eventually coalesce and form what Jung would later call the collective consciousness. But something also started to rise up into the collective in the late eighteenth century, and it might be best to begin our journey there.

While one could pick any point in history and declare it the commencement point of what I want to present to you, the role of Emanuel Swedenborg is a good place to start. This Swedish philosopher changed the way we looked at our divine nature in a manner that was, in ways, revolutionary. He called into curiosity the role of dreams as significant and mystical, but in a way that was less religious and more aligned with a spiritual sensibility that a contemporary person might easily appreciate. He also grabbed ahold of some scientific discoveries of the day, exploring anatomy and physiology, as well as dipping into an incipient study of what would turn into the science of neurons. Incidentally, this work is what eventually led science to understand that consciousness is somehow connected to the brain, and this is the scientific thread that got Freud's attention at the beginning of his career.

When Swedenborg was exploring dreams at a mystical level, Franz Mesmer was ten years old. Mesmer would grow up to generate the discovery that forever changed our sense of the human psyche. Mesmer was intensely curious about the workings of the energetic universe. As a physician, he focused on the body itself, but his work as an astronomer also put him into consideration about how we are all connected. He postulated that the human body is animated by a dynamic force, something he referred to as animal magnetism. His work exploring this energy and how it could be stimulated in people has become a common word: mesmerize. When we say that someone is mentally focused in one direction to the exclusion of other thoughts, we might say they are mesmerized. And though some of Mesmer's contributions would come into question, his work with this invisible energy allowed Scottish physician James Braid to expand those techniques just fifty years later. Braid called it hypnotism, and if this hadn't been introduced into the collective, Freud and Jung would never have been able to make the contributions they made.

Freud did not discover the unconscious mind, though he will be forever associated with creating the model of how we understand the structure of the unconscious that, with only minor modifications, we still use today. This would not have been possible without Mesmer and Braid, as it was through hypnosis that Freud first began to suspect that there were truly powerful ways that we could access the unconscious mind. It began with hypnosis, but this way of engaging with patients was soon discarded for what turned out to be something seemingly innocuous, but which was profoundly transformative. When people were given the opportunity to simply speak their conscious thoughts, Freud was able to glean things that were ultimately hints of complex emotions and thought patterns buried beneath the surface. This free association talking cure eventually led to discussions of the dreams patients were having. The resulting insights gained by exploring dreams were so revelatory and powerful for Freud, he ultimately dubbed dreams to be "the royal road to the unconscious mind." *The Interpretation of Dreams* was published in 1899, and the world has not been the same since.

Back to this missive. It arrived in a fascinating period. The Spiritualist movement, then in full force, would give way to a deeper understanding of the unconscious mind thanks to Freud and Jung, but not for at least another fifty years. At the time, dream interpretation was interesting to people curious about the potential to use dreams to predict the future. The second section of this book describes the technical elements of dream interpretation and guides the reader to create a series of ciphers and charts that will then allow the reader to interpret any dream. These charts are presented in a structure that uses planets and astrological signs as a guidepost. At the very top of the list, the reader is instructed to create these ciphers for themselves using the starting point suggested, with encouragement to allow intuition to assist the process.

The astrological elements of this book might seem organic to the modern reader, because since the middle of the twentieth century, most people living in Western culture not only know what sun sign they were born under, the notion that there are archetypes that govern personality through the principles of astrology is ubiquitous. But when this book was written, these ideas were not universal; that happened later, courtesy of the newspaper industry.

Before the 1930s, only an astrologer would know the zodiac with any sort of depth. But when Princess Margaret was born in England, a noted astrologer published a horoscope indicating a powerful and disruptive change would befall her and her family when she was a young girl. The abdication of her uncle was that disruption, and the London press went wild for the titillation that astrology might offer readers. It only took two decades. By the 1950s, every major newspaper in the world was carrying astrology columns using sun signs with the accompanying birth dates, and we now live in a world where this knowledge is commonplace. But in the late nineteenth century, this wisdom was in the domain of the mystic, further emphasizing that the likely audience for this book was probably specialized and included people who were diving deeply into the mysteries of the day in concomitance with the expanding interest in matters of the occult.

In modern dream interpretation through the lens of Jungian theory, and a branch known as depth psychology, we understand dreams to be a direct reflection of the psyche of the dreamer. While Freud may have first discovered the power that dreams have to reveal unconscious impulses, it was Jung who taught us to see dreams as a whole and complete inner landscape, where each person, being, animal, and scenario in the dream world is to be interpreted as an aspect of the dreamer's consciousness. One might think of this as the inner circle of interpretation. We also understand that dream content can reflect relationships and circumstantial challenges, and we work waking life conflicts out in the dream state. This might be best described as the outer circle of interpretation. While precognitive dreams, where dreams can offer intuitive information about future events, do exist, the current dominant sense of the value of dream interpretation is all about self-reflection.

What we have in this book is a significant reflection of a moment between. A few generations before, we were just discovering the potential of working with some of the ways we understand energy and connection. A few generations later, the field of modern psychology would open these mysteries up to us in a manner that helps us understand consciousness itself in our modern world. If you are drawn to this book, enjoy its quirky reflection of a previous moment in time, and may it inspire you to deepen your appreciation of the mysteries of the human psyche.

—Dr. Michael Lennox

THE DREAM BOOK

PREFACE

Are dreams fables? Some say they are, and that fables are nothing more than lies. This is a mistake, and an unfortunate error for anyone to fall into. Scores of notable people had remarkable dreams that related to their futures, and thus were prophetic in nature. You would be hard-pressed to find someone who has not, at some point in their life, had a remarkable and vivid dream that captured their imagination. But even more than this, dreams are *prophetic*.

You may wonder, what causes dreams? Many people say that our dreams are simply related to our bodies. For instance, if you overeat, you may find yourself gripped by a nightmare afterwards. This is often true, and I will try and explain it. The nightmare you experience is typically something terrifying coming upon you, or falling over you, and you feel it's impossible to escape. But who can say that this isn't a prophetic dream? It most certainly is. Many medical professionals would agree that an enormous dinner that leaves you miserably overfull will result in indigestion and discomfort. And the nightmare warned you of this: it tells you that something is coming upon you from which you cannot escape. What could be more clear?

Dreams, in my opinion, are caused by the *Soul.* When the physical and mortal parts of a person are, as it were, dead in sleep, the Soul shines forth, and produces certain impressions upon the brain. These are *dreams.* If dreams are not caused by some occult agency, why do you frequently dream of people, things, or places you've never seen, thought of, or heard about? *Something* cannot come from *nothing*; there must be a *cause.*

But, what is the purpose of dreams? Everything is sent for a purpose, and you cannot reasonably suppose that the Almighty Creator of all things permitted man to dream without a purpose. Believe me, reader, when I tell you that the more you study your dreams the more truth you will find in them—you will discover that they are prophetic, and, if you take note of them, you will save yourself a great deal of trouble.

—Raphael

INTRODUCTION

I've arranged this book in two parts—the first part is composed of a dream dictionary, giving meanings for many of the common objects and situations you might encounter in your dreams. The second part is an altogether different method of dream interpretation based on a system of ciphers. The second method of interpretation, through intuition and ciphers, is a less common method of interpreting dreams, but you may find it to be more accurate.

Not every dream needs to be interpreted, and I always ignore foolish dreams. Sometimes one dreams all kinds of nonsense, and I've invariably found that after that type of dream my life has gone on as usual, without a change. It's when you have a striking and vivid dream that the dream portends something. Foolish dreams are most likely caused by the brain without the co-operation of the Soul and it is easy to tell the difference between these mental wanderings and truly important dreams. In the same way, there's no doubt when one wakes up with a feeling of dread caused by the approach of a spiritual being whose nature is deeply uncanny and malevolent. Convulsive shuddering, when you are awake and perfectly healthy, is caused by a similar situation. There are millions of spiritual creatures walking the Earth that we can never see, since our senses are too blunt to perceive them. I will not say any more, lest I scare you. Only consult this book when your dreams are clear, vivid, and pointed, and you will not consult it in vain.

PART I
DREAM DICTIONARY

DICTIONARY

Abandon—To dream that you abandon a person is unfavorable; it suggests that you will lose friendships and goodwill. To dream that you are abandoned indicates trouble is coming.

Abbey—This indicates future comfort, peace of mind, and freedom from anxiety.

Abject—Dreaming that you are in a forlorn state indicates coming poverty; if, in your dream, you remain cheerful despite the situation, your poverty will only be for a season, and you will become prosperous.

Aboard—Dreaming of boarding a ship indicates success in your business or profession, and that you will become independent in a short period of time.

Abode—If you dream that you find yourself in a strange home, it foretells a sudden change in your fortune; if you are not allowed into the home or are put out, there is danger in your path.

Abortion—If a male dreams of this, trouble is approaching his partner. If a female dreams this, it is a dream of caution.

Above—To dream of seeing anything hanging above you indicates that your worldly prospects will improve; but if it falls and injures you, that is very bad.

Abroad—To dream of going abroad indicates a change in your situation in life.

Abscess—For a person to dream of having an abscess or sore foretells good fortune and good health that will be preceded by sickness.

Abscond—To dream that you run away is a sign that you are at risk of acting dishonorably. If you dream of another person fleeing, you will meet with a deceitful person—an unfaithful friend.

Absent friends—To dream of absent friends who are sick indicates bad news is approaching; to dream of friends who are healthy indicates that they are doing well; to dream of the death of a distant friend foretells good news.

Abundance—Dreaming of abundance indicates success in your plans, and that you are competent.

Abuse—To dream that someone is abusing you is a sure sign that you will quarrel with your lover or friend, and that someone has been talking badly about you. In business it indicates a loss or fraud.

Abyss—Trouble is coming. You will experience great difficulty and it will be hard to extricate yourself from the situation.

Accident—Dreaming that you have an accident or injure part of your body indicates a personal affliction, but one that you will recover from.

Accounts—If a businessperson dreams of keeping accounts it indicates loss due to the failure and bankruptcy of a business partner.

Accuse—To dream that you are accused of a crime and are guilty is a sign of great trouble; to dream that you are not found guilty indicates that your rival's plans will fail.

Ache—To dream that you have aches and pains indicates a temporary illness and small problems in your future.

Acorns—When you dream of acorns, it's a good sign; it indicates health, strength, and abundance; if single, you're likely to marry well. To businesspeople, it is the sign of prosperity and wealth. To those experiencing difficulties, it indicates quick relief.

Acquaintance—To dream of an acquaintance indicates their continued friendship.

Acquit—To dream that you are charged with a crime before a court and acquitted is a sure sign that you will prosper and your adversaries will not.

Acrobat—To dream of an acrobat indicates that you risk losing your life by some unforeseen accident, either by drowning, a car accident, or perhaps from a storm.

Actress—To dream of loving an actress is a sign that you will meet with trouble and adversities; but if you dream that you see her on stage, then you will find success.

Admire—To dream that you admire a person is a sign that

your partner loves you; and if single, that your lover is sincere. To dream that you are admired indicates that you will have numerous friends.

Admonish—For someone to dream that their sweetheart admonishes them or finds fault with them for being unfaithful indicates that they have a good relationship and that their love will increase.

Adopted—For a young person to dream that they are adopted by some wealthy person indicates they will lose either their father or mother, or some very near relative, who will leave behind someone who is dependent on their generosity.

Adornment—For someone to dream of being dressed in expensive clothing indicates financial loss and an inability to dress in decent clothes.

Adultery—Dreaming of being tempted to be unfaithful and avoiding it suggests that you will do well in life. But if you dream you are unfaithful, trouble is on its way.

Adversary—To dream you meet with an adversary and win indicates that you will overcome an obstacle to your happiness.

Adversity—To dream of being in hard circumstances is always a favorable dream; it generally indicates the reverse—prosperity.

Advice—To dream that you receive advice indicates difficulties. To dream that you are giving advice is a sign that you will be respected by your friends and acquaintances.

Advocate—To dream that you are an advocate is a sign that you will achieve high status and use your position to do good.

Affections—For a young person to dream that their affections are rejected by their lover signifies that their lover is faithful and their intentions are true.

Affliction—To the young, this indicates a change of residence, but not a good one.

Affluence—To dream of affluence is not favorable; it often indicates poverty.

Afraid—This indicates the opposite. In difficult situations you will be brave, not afraid.

Age—A dream about your age indicates sickness and an early death.

Agony—To dream of being in great pain, either mentally or physically, is an excellent dream. Prosperity, success, and good health will follow.

Alien—To dream that you are an alien, or alienated, is a dream of opposites. Instead of being an outsider, you will find friendship and love.

Alligator—This indicates a sly, crafty enemy; you should be cautious.

Almonds—To dream of eating sweet almonds indicates future enjoyment, most likely from traveling in a new country. If you enjoy the almonds, nearly every undertaking will be prosperous; if they taste bitter, your plans will fail.

Altar—To dream you are at an altar is a very unfavorable omen that indicates great adversity. If you are in business, you will suffer losses.

America—To dream that you have immigrated to this country indicates that you will stay in your current occupation and you will be successful.

Amputation—To dream that you have lost a limb is a warning of the death of someone close to you.

Anchor—To dream of an anchor in the water is a bad omen; it implies that your hopes and dreams will be disappointed. To dream of an anchor partially in the water and partially out foretells that you will soon go on a trip. To dream you see an anchor that is difficult to raise is a good sign that indicates continuing prosperity.

Angels—If you dream you are with them, it indicates that you will have strong relationships with lovely friends; that you will have prosperity, peace, and happiness. It is a good omen for lovers.

Anger—To dream you are angry with someone is a sign that that person is your best friend. Should you dream that your lover is angry with you, you can trust that they love you sincerely.

Annoy—To dream that you are annoyed indicates that you have enemies around you.

Ants—Dreaming of ants foretells that you will move to a large city. To those in love it foretells a quick marriage. It indicates good business and financial independence for the businessperson.

Anvil—To dream you hear the sound of the anvil is an excellent dream, signifying health, happiness, and wealth.

Anxiety—It means the opposite, and indicates that your current worry and anxiety will disappear.

Apes—To dream of apes is a bad omen, denoting a strange and spiteful rival who will deceive you.

Apparitions—*(See Ghost.)*

Applause—For a person to dream of being applauded by his friends indicates a sudden disparagement of his character, ending in lawsuits and fighting; the dream is very unfavorable.

Apples—This is a very good dream; it indicates a long and happy life, success in business and in love.

Apron—If you dream of a torn apron it is a sign of malicious gossip, caused by your own behavior; but if the apron is clean and undamaged, the dream is favorable.

Arm—To dream that your arms are weak is a sure sign that your health and fortunes are about to suffer. To dream that they are strong signals that unexpected success will come your way. To dream that your right arm is cut off indicates the death of some near relation; if it's your left, then the relative is female.

Arrow—To dream that you have been shot by an arrow is a bad omen. Someone does not wish you well.

Ascend—To dream that you climb a hill and reach the top indicates that you will overcome your difficulties.

Ashes—If you dream of ashes, misfortune and trouble are at hand; if you are a lover it indicates jealousy.

Ass—This indicates that whatever difficulty you are experiencing will come to an end if you are patient and humble.

Assassin—To dream of an assassin is a warning the dreamer should not ignore. Cut out all duplicitous friends from your life, don't lend anyone money, and be on your guard.

Atonement—To dream that you have to make amends for something you've done signifies that someone above you in social status will admire you.

Attorney—If a businessperson dreams they are speaking with an attorney, it indicates that the business will face obstacles. They will not have success.

Auction—For a person to dream that they attend an auction is very unfavorable; if you purchase something in your dream you can expect a loss; if you passed by the auction, you will achieve your dreams.

Baby—To dream that you are nursing a baby indicates sadness and disappointment in love.

Bachelor—Dreaming of a young bachelor signifies that you will soon meet a lover or friend. But to dream that you are speaking to an old bachelor is a sign that you are likely to be unlucky in love.

Back—To dream that you see your back indicates uneasiness and anxiety; if your back is broken or injured you will be mocked by your rivals. But to dream of your backbone indicates health and success in love and business.

Bacon—To dream of eating bacon predicts sorrow. To dream of buying it foretells the death of a friend.

Badger—If you dream of this animal, it's a good sign; it indicates a long life and great wealth that you will earn by hard work.

Baffled—To dream of being baffled or confused in your work is a good sign; if you are in love, you will win their affection and you will succeed in your business.

Bagpipes—This musical instrument always indicates extreme poverty, and that you will have to work hard all your life.

Bail—To dream you paid bail for a friend indicates that you will suffer when someone tries to take advantage of you.

Bakery—For a newlywed to dream of being in a bakery is very unlucky. It indicates that their partner will lose their job.

Baking—To dream of baking indicates sorrow and a death in the family.

Balcony—For someone to dream of being seated on a balcony with a lover indicates an interruption in their courtship, jealousy, or the lover's illness.

Bald—To dream of baldness indicates approaching sickness.

Ball—If you dream that you're dancing at a ball it signifies joy, happiness, and friendship. You will receive money or learn some good news.

Ballet—To dream you see a performance signifies that you will have attacks of pain or arthritis.

Balloon—To dream you go up in a balloon indicates you will chase after visionary goals in your work, but will not find success.

Banishment—To dream you are driven from your home, or exiled from your native country, is a very good dream. It indicates long life, abundance, peace, and honor.

Bank—If you dream of being a clerk in a bank, it indicates that you will lose your current job, and will have to take a less desirable position.

Bankrupt—To dream of bankruptcy is a warning. Don't do anything questionable that could hurt your reputation or make you lose the respect of your friends.

Banquet—For someone to dream they're at a banquet indicates prosperity and happiness are in store for them.

Bar—If you dream you are in a bar, it indicates that you will experience the anger of a rival. To dream that you are drinking with friends indicates deception by a flatterer.

Barefoot—To dream you go on a journey barefoot is a sign of prosperity; you will succeed and be generally fortunate in your life.

Barley fields—To dream of walking through a field of ripe barley indicates great trouble, the death of a dear relative, or sickness.

Barn—To dream you see a barn filled with corn indicates wealth, health, and long life; but if the barn is empty, you can expect the reverse.

Bath—To dream you see a bath indicates suffering. If you enter the bath and find it too hot, grief and sickness will find your family; but if you get into an extremely cold bath, it indicates joy and health.

Bathing—If you dream that you are bathing and the water is clear and transparent you will find success in love and prosperity in your work; but if the water is dirty and muddy you will experience poverty, poor health, and bad luck.

Bats—To dream of seeing a bat flying in the air indicates that you have an enemy or competitor. If it is flying during the daylight you need not fear, but if you dream of it flying by night you are in danger.

Battle—To dream of being in a battle implies conflict with neighbors, friends, or a lover. If you are victorious in your dream, it indicates that you will shrug off all your rivals' attempts to harm you.

Bay tree—To dream of a bay tree is an excellent sign for physicians and poets.

Beacon—For a person to dream that they see a beacon shining brightly on a dark night, either on sea or land, shows that they will be delivered from their worries and troubles.

Beans—To dream of beans is unfortunate. If you dream of eating them it foretells sickness. If you dream of seeing them growing, it foretells conflict with the people you love the most.

Bear—If you dream of seeing a bear, expect frustration and an adversary intent on doing you harm. If you dream that you are fighting a bear and kill it, that is a favorable sign indicating that you will overcome your adversary.

Beard—For a businessperson to dream of a beard predicts success and good fortune.

Beauty—To dream that you are beautiful is a sign of the opposite. It indicates that illness will ruin your looks and weaken you. To dream a friend is beautiful indicates their sickness. If you see you or your friend becoming more beautiful, it indicates death.

Bed—To dream of being in bed indicates a very early marriage; and to dream of making a bed indicates that you will move soon.

Bedroom—If you dream you are in a beautiful bedroom, it indicates that your circumstances are going to change for the better.

Beef—To dream of eating beef indicates that you will always have enough, though you may not be wealthy. If you dream of beef and cannot or do not eat it, that indicates that you will always be dependent on someone else's wealth.

Beer—Drinking good beer shows success in love and business; but if the beer is bad, expect trouble.

Bees—To dream of bees is good; it indicates that your work and business will be very successful. To the lover it indicates a happy marriage to a virtuous, hardworking, kind person.

Beetles—To dream that black beetles are creeping down your back indicates that someone is gossiping maliciously about you. If you kill the beetles in the dream, that means you will overcome the lies being told about you.

Beets—To dream you are eating beets indicates that your troubles are behind you and you will experience good luck.

Beheading—To dream you see anyone beheaded is a good sign, denoting love, courtship, and freedom.

Bellows—To dream that you stoke a fire with bellows signifies that you will never have what your heart desires and that trouble will surround you.

Bells—To dream of hearing the ringing of bells is a fortunate sign, indicating the arrival of good news. To a lover it represents an early marriage to a person who they love deeply. To people in business it promises that they will earn a large fortune.

Bequest—To dream of giving a bequest to others indicates trouble and loss for yourself.

Bet—To dream you make a bet with someone indicates that you will suffer from your own carelessness and encounter trouble that could have been avoided.

Bier—If in your dream you see a bier carried from your house, it signifies that someone in your family will soon be married.

Bigamy—If you dream that you are bigamous, it indicates that you will soon marry or, if you are already married, that your partner will outlive you.

Billiards—If you dream that you are playing billiards, it indicates that you will be placed in a difficult position that will be hard to extricate yourself from.

Birding—To dream you are watching birds indicates prosperity and gain; your work will be profitable.

Birds—For a wealthy person to dream of birds flying is very unlucky; it indicates a reversal of their circumstances. For a poor person to dream of birds indicates a change for the better. If the birds have beautiful plumage, it indicates the dreamer will become influential and socially successful.

Bird's nests—To dream of finding a bird's nest with eggs is a sign that you will inherit property. If there are chicks in the nest, the inheritance will be contested and you will lose it.

Birth—To dream of giving birth indicates health and growth.

Birthday—For a person to dream of their birthday indicates that someone mistakenly believes they are dead.

Biscuits—To dream of eating biscuits indicates that you will become ill.

Bishop—To dream of a bishop signifies that an important event is about to happen; you can expect sorrow, grief, and disappointment after this dream.

Bite—To dream you are bitten by an animal indicates you will suffer at the hands of a rival.

Blackberries—To dream that you are gathering blackberries yourself indicates approaching sickness. If you see others picking them, you will find you have adversaries and enemies where you least expect them.

Blankets—To dream you buy a blanket in the summer signifies that you will soon become sick; if you dreamt of buying it in the winter you will soon have a high fever.

Blasphemy—To dream you are cursing and swearing foretells serious misfortune; if you are the one being cursed at, then your wishes and hopes will be fulfilled.

Bleeding—To dream you are bleeding is a very unhappy dream, particularly if you dream that the bleeding does not stop, since that is a sign of chronic illness and suffering.

Blind—For someone who is in love to dream they are blind indicates that they made a bad choice in the object of their affection. If you dream of someone else being blind, this indicates that you have few true friends.

Blood—To dream of blood on yourself is a bad sign. If you see blood on someone else it indicates a sudden death in the family, loss of property, and severe disappointment. If you dream that your hands are bloody, you will be in danger of injuring someone. Be careful!

Blows—To dream you are being beaten indicates a reconciliation with your rivals. To dream you are hitting someone signifies that you must be careful of lawsuits.

Boat—If you dream that you are sailing in a boat or ship and the weather is beautiful with smooth water, it is a good omen, predicting you will be successful at work and find happiness in marriage. If the water is rough and choppy, you will have to work hard all your life. If you fall into the water, you will soon find yourself in great danger.

Bog—To dream that you are in a bog, sinking deep in the swamp, denotes misfortune and a loss of business.

Bones—Dreaming of bones indicates poverty. If the bones still have flesh on them, then you will grow rich by degrees and ultimately become wealthy. Dreaming of human bones foretells you will become wealthy through the death of a friend or family member.

Bonnet—To dream of receiving a bonnet means that you will have a new lover.

Books—To dream of books is a good sign; it indicates that your life will be very content and happy.

Boots—If you dream that you are wearing a new pair of boots and they hurt your feet, it is a sign you will encounter problems caused by your own foolishness.

Borrowing—To dream that you borrow anything is bad; it indicates trouble, sadness, and that you will have many enemies to contend with.

Bottle—To dream of a full bottle of wine indicates future prosperity; if the bottle is empty, it indicates that you have a rival who knows a secret that, if it is revealed, will cause you a great deal of trouble.

Bow and arrow—To dream that you are shooting a bow and arrow and hit your target indicates that your carefully thought out plans will succeed beyond your wildest dreams; if you miss the target, it shows that your plans are poorly thought out and will not work out.

Bowling—To dream you are bowling suggests that you will experience a reversal of fortune and will struggle with poverty.

Box—If you dream that you are looking for something in a box but cannot find it, it is an indication that you will be troubled by money problems.

Bouquet—To dream that you have received a bouquet from a lover indicates that you will have to wait a long time before you are married.

Boxwood—To dream of a boxwood plant implies long life and prosperity, with a happy marriage and large family.

Bracelet—To dream that you are wearing a bracelet means that you will soon marry a wealthy person. If you dream that you find a bracelet it is a sign that good fortune is coming to you.

Branch—If you dream that you see a tree full of branches, it indicates abundance and prosperity.

Bray—If you dream that you hear the braying of a donkey, it indicates that you will soon learn of the death of an eccentric celebrity.

Bread—To dream of seeing bread is a sign that you are capable and competent. If you dream of eating good bread, you will enjoy good health and a long life. If the bread is burned or bad, it generally predicts a funeral. To dream of baking bread is also bad, indicating sorrow and sadness.

Break—To dream of anything breaking is unlucky. If you dream of breaking a limb, it is a sign of approaching sickness. If you dream of breaking tables or chairs, or any kind of furniture, it indicates bankruptcy. If you dream of breaking a window, it warns of a robbery or fire. If you dream of breaking a mirror, it implies the death of a relative, neighbor, or friend. To dream of breaking pottery or glass indicates theft by an employee, and if you dream of breaking your wedding ring, it portends the death of your spouse.

Breakfast—To dream that you are eating your breakfast indicates that you will do something that will cause you grief and sorrow.

Breath—To dream you are out of breath, or have difficulty breathing, is a sign that your health is poor.

Brewing—If you dream that you are brewing beer, you can expect a visit from a distant friend. It indicates that you have put great effort into a good cause and that you will succeed—there will be doubt and trouble for a short time, but it will end in happiness.

Briars—To dream that you are scratched by briars and brambles is a very unlucky dream; it indicates that your life will have many difficulties and struggles. If you dream you are not scratched by the briars you will face obstacles, but they will be short-lived.

Bride, Bridesmaid, or Bridegroom—This is a dream that means the opposite of what you expect. To dream that you are in any of these roles is unlucky: it is a sure sign of grief and disappointment.

Bridge—To dream that you are crossing a bridge during the day predicts that your situation and circumstances will change. If someone interrupts you as you cross, it implies that your lover will deceive you; but if you cross the bridge freely, you will succeed in your goals and prosper.

Broth—To dream you are eating broth indicates good fortune, success, and happiness.

Brothers—To dream you see your siblings signifies that you will live to a good old age, but you can expect a death in the family soon.

Bugle—To dream that you are playing this instrument is a happy sign, meaning strong friendship and kindness from your relatives. To dream of hearing a bugle indicates unexpected good news.

Bugs—To dream of these nasty creatures indicates sickness, and many rivals that are seeking to overcome you. To a businessperson, it indicates that they have employees who are seeking to rob them.

Buildings—If you dream of seeing a large number of new buildings, it indicates that you will soon move to a distant place where you will be far happier, and escape the influence of your adversaries. If the buildings are large and lovely, you will be prosperous and happy; if they are palaces, it promises wealth and honor; but if they appear small and dilapidated, you will be impoverished.

Bull—To dream that you are pursued by an angry bull indicates that you have violent enemies, and that they are spreading false rumors about you. If you are in love, your partner will be in some kind of danger and will only barely escape misfortune.

Bulldog—To dream you meet with this faithful breed of dog is a sign that friends you thought had forgotten you will come back into your life. They will help you financially if need be. But if the bulldog bites you, expect that an enemy will cause you trouble.

Burden—To dream you have a heavy burden and cannot carry it signifies that others will depend on you for support.

Burglars—To dream that burglars enter your home and you fight them off is a sign that you will vanquish your enemies; but if they beat you and take your things, it is a very bad sign. Loss and legal troubles will follow.

Burial—To dream that a burial procession passes by you implies that you will hear some news. To dream you bury your best friend indicates you will have good news from friends or relatives who are abroad.

Burns—A dream to the contrary, implying health, happiness, and warm friendship.

Butchers—To dream you see a butcher is a very unlucky dream; be careful of injury. If you see the butcher cutting up meat, some of your friends will find themselves in serious trouble.

Butter—To dream of butter, in any way, shape, or form, is a good dream, and indicates joy and good food.

Buttermilk—To dream of drinking buttermilk implies you will be disappointed in love.

Buttons—If you dream of colorful or shiny buttons it is good; if they are old or broken, it indicates misfortune. If the button is covered, it means sadness. If you dream you've lost a button from your clothing, it means you will not live long and will lose money in your business.

Cab—To dream of riding in a cab indicates a short sickness with a quick recovery brought about by a change of climate. It also indicates that your wealth will grow.

Cabbage—To dream of cutting cabbages indicates that your wife, or lover, or husband, as the case may be, is very jealous of you. If you dream of eating cabbage, it indicates that the object of your affections will become sick.

Cabin—To dream you are in the cabin of a ship signifies trouble in marriage.

Cage—To dream that you see birds in a cage is a sign that you will marry young and have a happy marriage. If you dream you see a cage where the birds have flown free, it is a sign that your lover will forsake you. To dream of seeing a person letting a bird escape from its cage is a sign of an elopement.

Cakes—If you dream of oat cakes, it indicates health and strength; of sweet cakes, coming joy; if you dream of making spice cakes or bread, an approaching marriage.

Calf—For someone to dream they see a calf when out walking with a lover indicates that they will marry.

Called—For a person to dream she hears her name called aloud is a significant dream. It is a warning to attend to whatever you have been neglecting.

Calm—To dream of calm after a storm indicates that friends will reconcile; the end of trouble, and the beginning of peace.

Camels—To dream of these wonderfully hardy and patient creatures indicates that you will carry an almost overwhelming burden and confront much hardship in your life, all of which you will bear heroically.

Camp—For someone to dream they are in an army camp indicates that they will be involved with a soldier.

Campaign—To dream you are part of a military or political campaign indicates you will be called upon to care for a sick friend.

Canal—To dream you are walking along a canal full of muddy water signifies that someone will try to do you harm; if the waters are clear, then you will enjoy prosperity and happiness.

Canary—If you dream that you hear a canary sing it indicates that you will marry happily.

Cancer—To dream you have cancer in any part of your body is good; it promises good health and strength.

Candles—To dream you see a candle burning brightly portends that you will receive good news; but if you dream that you see a candle snuffed or blown out, it indicates the death of a friend or relative.

Candy—To dream you are eating candy signifies that trouble is coming upon you; someone in your family will be taken ill.

Canker—If a person dreams that his child has a canker sore it indicates that they will grow up to be an eloquent speaker, possibly an actor or singer.

Cannon—To dream of hearing a cannon blast indicates war for your country, and personal trouble and frustration.

Cannonball—To dream you see a cannonball indicates misfortune, trouble, and a period of anxiety.

Canoe—To dream you are in a canoe on a river is unfavorable. It means you will always have to fight your way through life: friends will refuse to help you, and no one but your partner will support you.

Canopy—To dream you are sitting under a canopy indicates you will soon have to move to a more affordable home.

Captive—To dream of being held captive is a sign of coming bankruptcy. It is also a sign of an unhappy marriage due to the bad temper of your spouse.

Cards—To dream you are playing cards indicates a quick marriage. If the cards are mostly diamonds, your partner will be irritable; if hearts, your marriage will be very happy; if clubs, your partner will be wealthy; if spades, you and your children will be unhappy.

Carpet—To dream that you are in a carpeted room indicates that you will become wealthy.

Carriage—If you dream of riding in a carriage, it is a dream to the contrary and indicates that you will become poor.

Carrots—To dream of this vegetable indicates profit, gain, and success in any lawsuits.

Cart—To dream of riding in a cart indicates that you will come down in the world and experience many hardships. To dream of driving a cart indicates business in your future.

Carving—To dream that you are carving meat for others indicates that you will be a benefactor. If you are carving meat for yourself, you will find success in your work.

Castle—To dream of being in a castle indicates you will receive an inheritance. If you dream of seeing the castle from a distance, it means you will expect an inheritance, but not receive it. If you dream of leaving a castle it indicates heavy losses.

Caterpillars—To dream you see caterpillars indicates trouble and misfortune caused by secret enemies.

Cathedral—To dream that you are in a cathedral indicates that you will enjoy an income that allows you to travel.

Cats—An unlucky dream, denoting treachery and deceit. If a lover dreams of cats, it is a sign that their beloved is sly and deceitful. If a businessperson dreams of cats, it indicates untrustworthy employees. To dream that you kill a cat is an indication that you will identify your rivals and derail their plans; if the cat scratches you, it is very unlucky.

Cattle—If you dream of cattle grazing in a pasture, it is a sign of prosperity and affluence. If you dream of herding cattle, it portends that, if you work diligently, you will be wealthy. Black cows with long horns predict numerous and violent enemies.

Cauliflower—To dream of eating cauliflower is a sign of sickness, but if you see it growing that indicates prosperity.

Cave—For a person to dream they are in a cave indicates they will suffer from scandal and gossip.

Celery—To dream you eat celery indicates you will have strong, robust health.

Cellar—To dream of being in a full cellar indicates prosperity and success; if it is empty, that shows loss and poverty. If you are locked in the cellar that is a sign of misfortune.

Chains—To dream you see chains is a sign that enemies are planning to harm you, but that you will avoid them. If you dream that you are restrained by chains, it indicates that you will experience hard trials, but will overcome them.

Chaff—This dream indicates that your plans are not well thought out and will fail.

Chapel—To dream that you are at service in a chapel, or in another place of worship, is a bad sign; you will have trouble and disappointment at every step.

Charity—If a rich person dreams he is charitable, it indicates trouble and a loss of fortune. If a lover dreams it, they will bestow their affections on an unworthy person.

Chastise—For a parent to dream they chastise their children for disobedience indicates that they will be obedient and kind.

Cheated—To dream you have been cheated should put you on your guard at work and in business or you will be stolen from or defrauded.

Cheese—To dream of cheese indicates that your lover is deceptive and unfaithful. If the cheese is spoiled, it indicates petty, meddling people will annoy you. To dream of eating cheese indicates regret for having acted foolishly.

Cherries—*(See Fruit.)*

Chess—If you dream you are playing chess with an acquaintance it indicates you will fall out with some of your friends. If you dream you win, you will succeed over your rivals; but if you lose, then they will succeed instead.

Chestnuts—To dream of eating chestnuts indicates that the unwed will be married. To the married it indicates coming sickness.

Chickens—To dream of a hen and chickens predicts bad luck. To a farmer, it indicates a bad season.

Chicks—For a parent to dream they see a brood of chicks under the wings of a hen indicates that, in spite of all their careful parenting, some of their children will be led astray.

Children—This is a lucky dream, and promises success at work and prosperity; to dream that you see your child die is a dream to the contrary—it means your child will recover.

Cholera—To dream that you have this disease signifies that some accident will occur to you soon.

Church—To dream that you go to church in mourning indicates a wedding; if you go in white, it indicates a funeral. At all times it indicates disappointment.

Churchyard—To dream of being in a churchyard indicates that you will attend a wedding. You will enjoy good health for some time.

Clergyman—*(See Pastors.)*

Climbing—To dream you are climbing signifies you will be very successful throughout your life. If you reach the top, you will overcome all of your troubles; but if you wake up before reaching it, you will be disappointed; if you fall, you will lose your current status in life.

Clock—To dream you hear the clock strike indicates a quick marriage. To dream that you are counting the hours before noon indicates much happiness; but if you are counting the hours after noon, you will encounter misfortune and danger.

Clothes—To dream that you have lovely clothing means the opposite. It indicates want and a scarcity of clothes. If you dream you have no clothes that means you will have everything you need.

Clothes (White)—To dream you are dressed in white is a sure sign of success in business, or any honorable undertaking; you will become very popular.

Clothes (Black)—If you go to a funeral in black, it indicates a marriage. But to dream of black apparel on ordinary occasions is unlucky. It indicates sickness to yourself or your family, and you will lose someone dear to you.

Clothes (Blue or purple)—This indicates prosperity, happiness, and respect from people you want to impress; success in business, the affirmation of friends, and a great deal of traveling.

Clothes (Scarlet)—By dreaming of this color you've been warned that you will experience sickness, sadness, the loss of friends, and conflict.

Clothes (Crimson)—To dream of being dressed in crimson indicates that the dreamer will enjoy a long, happy life.

Clothes (Various colors)—To dream you are dressed in a variety of colors indicates that you will have mixed fortunes throughout your life.

Clothes (Someone else's)—To see someone else in the colors described above means that the same fortune applies to them.

Clothes (New clothes)—To dream you are dressed in new clothes is a favorable sign; it predicts success in your plans.

Clouds—To dream of dark clouds suspended over you indicates that you will have to pass through overwhelming sorrow. But if the clouds break and move away, your struggles will pass away as well and you will be successful.

Clover—If you are in a field of clover, it is an omen that you will do well, enjoy good health, and be very happy. If you are in love, this is an ideal sign—everything you undertake will succeed.

Coal mine—To dream that you are near a coal mine indicates that you will be exposed to danger. To dream that you are in a coal mine is a sign that you will not escape the danger.

Coals—To dream of coals indicates trouble; death to yourself or a relative; and forewarns you of poverty and prison. To dream the coals are burning clear and bright is good.

Coat—To dream your coat is torn indicates serious trouble; be especially careful of your behavior after this dream.

Coffee—This dream is favorable. It indicates contentment in life, prosperity, and a happy marriage.

Coffin—It is a bad dream. This is a sign of the death of a close friend or of your lover.

Cold—This indicates a comfortable life; kind and loving friends.

Collar—Dreaming of an iron collar on your neck shows poverty and imprisonment.

Combat—To dream of combat with anyone indicates rivalry, and that you will seek revenge. If you dream that you win the fight, it is a sign that your love will continue to be faithful to you.

Comets—They portend chaos among nations, war, famine, and plague, and even cold-blooded murder. Everyone who dreams this can expect misfortune.

Command—If you dream you can command anyone, it signifies your star will rise in life. To dream you see someone else giving orders indicates authority and anger.

Companion—To dream of your companion indicates abiding friendship.

Complexion—To dream your complexion is good shows sickness; but if it's bad, it indicates health. The same with others. It is a dream of opposites.

Concubine—If you dream of speaking to a concubine, it indicates that you have strayed from the moral path.

Concert—To dream of a concert denotes discord and strife among family members.

Conscience—To dream your conscience accuses you of something you've done indicates that you will be honest with yourself and that your conscience will prick you when you do wrong.

Convicted—*(See Accuse.)*

Cooking—Dreaming of cooking indicates an enjoyable party, and a friend's wedding.

Corks—To dream that you are corking bottles indicates that soon you will have to entertain. If you are uncorking a bottle, it is a sign that a good friend will visit.

Cornfield—To dream of cornfields or corn is a favorable omen; it predicts health, a happy family, profitable work, and great wealth. Your risks will reward you. If the corn is ripe, your fortune is at hand; if it's unripe, you must wait before good fortune arrives.

Corpse—To dream you see a corpse predicts a rushed, poorly considered marriage, in which both parties will be very unhappy.

Cotton—To dream you see a large amount of cotton indicates that market demand will wain and those who work in production will struggle to make a profit.

Cough—To dream you are troubled with a violent cough indicates you will be healthy and have strong lungs.

Courtship—For a young person to dream of courtship means they will not marry.

Cow—To dream that you are pursued by a cow indicates you have an enemy; if you escape it, you will overcome them. To dream of milking a cow is a sign of abundance.

Cowslips—If you dream you see cowslips in full bloom, you can expect a sudden change in your fortune.

Cradle—For a parent to dream a cradle is broken indicates their youngest child will become ill.

Crabs—To dream of a crab indicates a reversal of fortune; and to a sailor, danger of shipwreck and drowning.

Crawl—To dream you are crawling on the floor is bad; it denotes future loss and trouble. To dream that you are crawling on the roof of a house is a warning to be careful.

Crew—To dream you see the crew of a vessel hard at work reefing their sails indicates storms at sea and that one of your friends will suffer an accident relating to water.

Cries—If you dream you hear a cry of distress, expect to hear glad news from a friend. If it's a cry of joy, look out for the death of a relative. If the cry is full of despair, it indicates that you will gain wealth through speculation.

Crown—To dream that you wear a royal crown is a dream to the contrary; it indicates that you will lose social status. To dream that you give someone else a crown shows that you will rise to independence.

Crows—This is a sign of a funeral.

Crutches—To dream you are walking on crutches is very unfavorable; if you see another walking on them, it signifies that a friend will be injured and will be obliged to use them.

Crystal—Dreaming of crystal indicates that someone you respect will give into temptation and it will be their downfall.

Cuckoo—This dream indicates temporary disappointments in love, even a breakup. If you dream that you hear a cuckoo, and it stutters, this indicates that you will not succeed in business or love.

Cucumbers—It indicates health for the ill to dream of cucumbers. To a single person, an agreeable marriage.

Currants—*(See Fruits.)*

Dairy—To dream that you are in a dairy making butter indicates that you will be very fortunate in your business concerns and that you will marry a plain person.

Daisy—To dream of daisies in spring or summer is good and indicates prosperity, but to dream of daisies in winter is very unfortunate.

Damsons—If you dream of this kind of fruit when it is out of season, it indicates trouble and frustration.

Dance—This is a favorable dream; it indicates that you will be respected and honored and that you will meet your goals; in love you will win the hand of a valuable person.

Danger—If you dream you are in danger, it warns you to be careful in business; if you get hurt, you will suffer a loss.

Dark—If you dream that you are in darkness and cannot find your way, it indicates a negative change in your situation. But if you dream that you emerge from the darkness and see the sun, it indicates your escape from adversity; you will be happy, and regain your reputation.

Dead—To dream of your relatives and friends who are dead indicates that you or a relative is suffering deeply. If you dream that they are happy, it is a good omen.

Death—This a dream to the contrary; it predicts a long, happy life. To the single person it indicates a happy marriage. However, if a sick person dreams of death, it portends death.

Debt—To dream you are in debt and cannot pay indicates wealth and prosperity; but if you dream you have plenty of money to pay your debts it is bad luck and implies loss in business.

Decorate—To dream you bedeck yourself in gorgeous clothing indicates that you will lack beautiful clothing. To dream you are decorating a room signifies poverty and ill fortune.

Deer—This is an unfavorable dream; it indicates you will take part in squabbling and conflict. It's a bad dream for businessmen, sailors, and officials.

Defraud—*(See Fraud.)*

Delicate—If you are sick and dream you have delicate health, it signifies a speedy recovery. To a healthy person it indicates even greater strength and robustness.

Delight—To dream you are delighted by something signifies that sorrow and trouble will shortly arrive from an unexpected source.

Demand—To dream that an unfair demand is placed on you warns you to beware of friends who are striving to undercut your business relationships.

Desert—To dream that you are traveling across a desert is a sign of a difficult and dangerous journey, especially if you dream that the weather is rainy and windy. If you see the sun shine, your journey will be safe and prosperous.

Despair—To dream you feel despair signifies you will soon have cause to rejoice; your fortune will take a turn for the better.

Detective—To dream a detective is trying to apprehend you indicates that you will go through life with a good reputation.

Devil—This is a hard dream, and foretells loss, sickness, and misfortune.

Devotion—To dream that you are devoted is a sign of good health and happiness.

Diadem—For a person to dream that they are wearing a diadem indicates a fall in their circumstances. They will struggle to find happiness and honor.

Diamond—This dream indicates dependable wealth and the granting of your wishes.

Dice—To dream that you are playing dice is a sign of great change in your business and circumstances; it means that your life will be very variable with highs and lows.

Difficulty—To dream you are experiencing difficulty or any kind of personal danger is favorable, as it indicates the opposite.

Digging—To dream you are digging in clean earth indicates thrift and good luck; if the ground is wet or muddy, it indicates trouble. If you are searching for gold and find large nuggets it indicates good fortune, but if you do not find much, it indicates disappointment.

Dinner—If you dream that you are eating dinner, it foretells hard times and obstacles. You will not be comfortable in married life.

Dirt—To dream that your body or clothes are dirty indicates sickness and sorrow. It also implies that your reputation will be damaged. To dream that someone throws dirt on you is a sign that your enemies will try to injure your character.

Disaster—It is a dream of opposites; you will hear that good friends have been successful. To dream of disaster at sea portends a prosperous voyage. It is a favorable dream for a person of business.

Disease—If you are sick, to dream of disease is a sign of recovery; to the young it is a warning against bad company and self-indulgence.

Disgrace—To dream that you disgrace yourself through some thoughtless act signifies that you will behave wisely and build a good reputation.

Dislike—If you dream you are disliked and this troubles you, then an enemy or rival will do you harm; if in your dream you are not bothered by others' dislike, but feel defiant instead, that is a sign that you will triumph over all your rivals.

Dispute—Disputes always foretell fighting and conflict, and setbacks in your business; but they will be short-lived and you will succeed in the end.

Distance—To dream that you are far from your friends is a sign of fighting and estrangement in the family. To dream of a distant friend means that you will soon hear from them.

Ditch—To dream of ditches is unfavorable: it indicates danger, losses, injury, and many adversaries working against you.

Divorce—This is a dream to the contrary. If a married person dreams of divorce, it is a sign of the fidelity of their partner, and that they have no cause for jealousy.

Docks—To dream that you are standing by a dock indicates you will hear good news from abroad.

Doctor—To dream of visiting a doctor indicates your health is good, and that you will have no need of medical care for some time.

Dogs—If you dream that a dog cuddles with you, you will meet faithful friends. But if he bites you, your best friend will become your greatest enemy. If the dog barks at you, you will quarrel with your friend or lover.

Dolphins—This is not a good dream. It indicates the death of a friend at sea. If you travel, it indicates great danger.

Donkey—To dream you are riding on a donkey indicates that your social status will rise. To hear a donkey bray indicates the death of an eccentric celebrity. To dream you are kicked by one indicates you have rivals who will seek to do you harm.

Doves—This is a fortunate dream. It indicates progressive prosperity in business, the love of friends, and peace in the family. If you hear the call of a turtledove, it is an omen of the death of a dear friend. If you dream of a dove being shot and see it fall to the ground, it is a sign of your own death.

Dragon—Should you dream of a dragon, prepare yourself for an unexpected change in your situation and circumstances.

Dreams—For a person to dream they are telling their dream to another indicates that something unexpected is about to take place.

Dress—To dream of buying a dress indicates a promotion, and that your wishes will come true.

Drink—To dream that you are drinking at a fountain is a sign of happiness and joy. If the water is muddy, it indicates approaching trouble. If you are thirsty and cannot find water, it is a sign that you will have to endure times of trouble without help.

Driving—If you dream of driving, expect a loss in business. To dream that someone is driving you is a good sign; it foretells a marriage.

Drown—To dream that you are drowning indicates overwhelming difficulties, loss in business, and even death. If you dream you are drowning and are rescued, it is a sign that friends will help you in your difficulties and sorrows.

Drum—To dream you hear the sound of a drum is a sign of national and personal turmoil. The country will be at war.

Drunk—To dream that you are drunk indicates you will fall into dire straits, and that you will be reckless with yourself, your reputation, and your livelihood.

Ducks—If you see ducks flying, it's an omen of increasing wealth; if you see them swimming on water, it is a good sign for artists, businessmen, and lovers.

Dunghill—To dream you stand on a dunghill is very favorable; it indicates success and prosperity.

Dust—To dream that you are almost blinded with dust indicates the failure of your business, and the separation of your family. But if in your dream you manage to escape the dust, you will recover in your life as well.

Eagles—To dream you see an eagle soaring very high in the air signifies prosperity, wealth, and honor; to the lover it indicates success and a happy marriage. To see an eagle on a church steeple indicates the dreamer will make their fortune overseas.

Earthquake—This foretells trouble for the dreamer: it indicates loss in business or work, bereavement, and separation and conflict within a family.

Earwig—An enemy! He will threaten to undermine your happiness.

Eating—To dream that you are eating alone is a bad omen; it indicates family fighting, sickness, a breakup between lovers, business losses, a bad harvest, and a shipwreck or accident. To dream you are eating with other people indicates friendship and considerable success in your work or profession.

Eclipse—This indicates that, regardless of what your wish is, it will not come true.

Education—To dream of education in any way indicates that you will find literary fame.

Eels—To dream of eels warns you to beware of risky endeavors. If the eels escape from you, expect a loss; but if you manage to keep hold of them, you will enjoy honor and happiness in marriage.

Eggs—To dream of seeing a large number of eggs indicates success in trade and in love. To dream that the eggs are rotten indicates unfaithful friends and lovers. To dream of eating eggs is a sign of great happiness to come.

Elderberries—*(See Fruit.)*

Elephant—To dream of an elephant indicates health and strength and that you will be a respected member of society.

Elopement—To dream that you are eloping with your lover indicates an unhappy marriage. If you dream that your lover has eloped with someone else, the sooner you end the relationship the better because your rival will likely steal your beloved's affections. To dream of a relative eloping indicates that they will be married. To dream of a friend or acquaintance eloping is a sign of a sudden death.

Embroidery—To dream of embroidery indicates that those who appear to love you are deceitful.

Emerald—To dream you purchase an emerald signifies that the extravagance of a loved one will cause you trouble.

Employment—To dream that you need employment is a sign of prosperity. To dream that you are very busy at work is a sign that you will have nothing to do. To dream that you employ others is a sign that, if you are not mindful, you will cause them harm. This is a dream of opposites.

Enemy—To dream you talk to an enemy is a sign to be careful of them. To dream you fight with them and they win signifies a misfortune that has been approaching for a long time, but if you best them, it is favorable.

Enlist—To dream that you enlist in the army signifies you will leave your current job, and will receive a good offer from another place.

Entertainment—To dream of entertainment is the sign of a coming celebration. If you were delighted in your dream you will soon marry. It is a good dream for a businessperson. To the sailor it means a successful voyage and safe return and to the soldier, safety in battle.

Envy—To dream that you are envied is a sign that you will be admired and loved, and that your rivals will not be a threat to you. This is a dream of opposites.

Epicure—To dream that you see an epicure is a sign that you will see a sick friend; if you dream that you are an epicure, it indicates you will become sick.

Ermine—To dream you see anyone wearing fur indicates that you will become an important and honored person. If you dream that you are wearing ermine, it indicates a great and magnificent future is waiting for you.

Escape—To dream that you try to escape from some type of danger and cannot indicates continued trouble. To dream that you escape from sickness, an enemy, fire, or water is a good sign; you will experience a hard season, but it will not last.

Estate—For someone to dream that they inherit a great estate means that their spouse will be lazy and worthless.

Evening—To dream of the evening is a sign of an early death. It indicates the decline of life, and the approach of the long night of eternity.

Evergreens—Lasting happiness! Lasting love! Lasting honor! Domestic bliss! Everything you undertake will meet with success.

Evil spirits—*(See Ghosts.)*

Execution—To dream of an execution shows changes in your business; if you feel horrified in your dream, expect losses.

Exile—If you dream that you are banished, it implies that you will travel a great deal.

Eye—To dream you see a person with a sore eye indicates sickness or deception; with only one eye, disappointment.

Fables—If you dream that you are reading, telling, or listening to a fable, it indicates that you will have good friends with whom you will enjoy a strong relationship.

Faces—If you dream that you see your own face in a mirror, it is a sign that your secret plans will be discovered, and that you will be judged. If you see strange faces in your dream, it means that you will move from your present home and find a new social circle.

Factory—To dream you're inspecting a factory indicates that your work or business will be successful.

Failure—To dream that you fail in business; that you fail to find love; that you do not meet your goals is a dream of opposites; it indicates that if you proceed wisely you will succeed in everything you do.

Fair—It is very unlucky to dream you are at a fair as it portends negligence and failure in your work and unreliable friends.

Fairy—People who are very poor have dreamed of fairies and afterward become very rich. The working man who dreams this dream will rapidly increase his wealth.

Falcon—This is a very bad dream. There is a rival in your life who is full of envy and will injure you with their words.

Fall—To dream that you fall from a rock, from a tree, or the edge of a precipice indicates a loss of social status and of property. To a businessperson, it indicates a failing business, embarrassment, etc. To the sailor it indicates a stormy voyage and shipwreck.

False—To dream of false or untrustworthy friends means exactly the reverse; you will have true, firm, and lasting friendships.

Fame—For a young person to dream they become famous indicates a coming failure in business.

Famine—This is a dream of opposites, denoting national prosperity and individual comfort, wealth, and happiness.

Farm—To dream that you are buying a farm indicates that you will advance in your career. If you dream of visiting a farm and buying their products, it is a sign of good health.

Father—To dream of your father indicates that he loves you; if he is dead, it is a sign of sadness or sickness.

Favor—For a person to dream he is in the good graces of someone above him in social class indicates that he will become a philanthropist in his old age.

Fawn—For a young person to dream of a young deer is a sign of fickleness and unreliability.

Fear—To dream that you are scared by some mysterious event is very favorable. It means you will receive an inheritance from a wealthy person.

Feasting—This is an unfavorable dream, predicting disappointment, rivalry, and sadness.

Feeble—*(See Sickness.)*

Feet—To dream that you are washing your feet in a river or fountain signifies trouble and unrest; to dream that someone touches the soles of your feet indicates that someone will betray you. Beware!

Fence—If you dream that you've climbed a high fence, it signifies you will suddenly rise in life; if you crawl under a fence, you will behave in a shameful, degrading way.

Ferret—If you dream you see one of these animals, it indicates rivals and enemies; and if it bites you and draws blood, they will cause you a lot of trouble.

Festival—To dream you are at a festival is a sign of sadness, sickness, and sorrow.

Fever—To dream that you have a fever indicates instability and change in your work and circumstances. Sometimes you will be wealthy, then poor.

Fiddle—This dream is a sign of prosperity and delight. You will receive good news from a beloved, distant friend. To dream that you are tuning and playing the fiddle indicates you will marry quickly. If in your dream the strings break, you will never wed.

Fields—To dream that you are walking in green fields is a sign of prosperity and good luck, whether in work or in love. To dream of walking in withered or scorched fields indicates coming poverty. To dream that you are in clover fields or barley and wheat fields and the crops are flourishing indicates that you will enjoy powerful connections and become very wealthy. If you dream that you are in a freshly plowed field it indicates that success is coming, but you will have to make many sacrifices and be tireless in your pursuit of your goal.

Fiend—*(See Ghost.)*

Fighting—This dream indicates disagreements and quarrels in families. It also indicates misunderstandings among lovers and possibly temporary separation. If you dream that a person fights you and beats you, it is a sign that your competitors will win over you; if you beat your opponent, then you will overcome your rivals as well.

Figs—*(See Fruit.)*

Filberts—*(See Fruit.)*

Fingers—If you dream you cut your fingers and they bleed, it shows that you will do something to harm your own interests; if another cuts your finger, you can expect injury from an enemy or rival.

Fire—It is a sign of health and great happiness, a loving family, and warm friends. But if you dream that you are burned by the fire, it is a sign of coming catastrophe.

Fish—To dream of seeing a number of fish indicates that you will be happy and relatively well off financially. If you dream that a fish slips through your fingers, it indicates a loss of status, friends, and lovers.

Fishing—To dream you catch a fish is a sign of prosperity;

but if you catch nothing, then your goals will remain unmet.

Fits—To dream of having a fit implies health, success, and happiness.

Flag—To dream you see a flag waving warns you of danger from a rival, or sickness. To dream you carry a flag indicates you will become distinguished and respected.

Flames—If in your dreams you see flames ascending into the air it indicates that your friends are speaking poorly of you; if the flames burn you the situation is very bad.

Fleas—To dream that you are annoyed by fleas indicates that you are being harmed by enemies or rivals; business will be bad, friends will be deceitful, and lovers unfaithful.

Floating—To dream you are floating on water is a fortunate dream, denoting long life and happiness; but if you sink, it is very, very bad, and indicates certain poverty.

Floods—For sailors to dream of a flood is a favorable dream, denoting a safe and successful voyage, but to ordinary people it indicates bad health and lawsuits that are not decided in your favor.

Flour—To dream you buy flour is a bad dream, denoting sickness, or the death of a near friend.

Flowers—To dream that you are gathering beautiful and sweet-smelling flowers is an indication of prosperity; you will be very lucky in everything you undertake. If in your dream you gather the flowers into a bouquet, it portends a very happy marriage. If you dream of withered flowers, it is a sign of failing health and approaching death.

Flying—To dream of flying indicates that you will escape many difficulties and dangers. It indicates success in trade and in love. If you dream that you are trying to fly higher and higher, it is an indication that you will aspire to something you will never reach.

Fog—Indicates great uncertainty. You have asked your friends for help, but they will never give it. You take a risk on the stock market and it might ruin you. You are hoping for good health, but it is unreliable. The dream is bad. If you dream that the fog clears away and the sun shines, your luck will be reversed and uncertainty will vanish.

Forest—For a person to dream that he or she is in a lush, green forest is good, denoting extraordinary success and prosperity. But if you lose yourself in the forest, be careful; it implies losses.

Fortress—If you dream you are locked in a fortress, it indicates your goals in life will be negatively influenced by the plans of others. To dream you have locked someone else in a fortress indicates that you should look for valuable business opportunities.

Fortune—It is a dream of opposites. If you dream that someone has left you a fortune, it is a sign that they will not. If you dream that your friend received a fortune, it is a sign of their coming poverty. It is a bad dream.

Fountain—To dream you see a muddy fountain indicates

trouble. To see a crystal clear, overflowing fountain indicates abundance and freedom from want.

Fowl—To dream of fowl indicates moderate comfort in worldly things; but it indicates that in love you will find gossip and deception.

Fox—If you dream of a fox, you have a sly, lurking enemy—a business competitor determined to undermine your interests, or a rival in love looking to replace you. If you are involved in a lawsuit, your lawyer is double dealing and you will suffer for it.

Fratricide—Whoever dreams they are guilty of this crime can consider themselves very unfortunate. They will never find success.

Fraud—If you charge someone with committing fraud, you will discover that you have been robbed by that person. To dream that you have committed a fraud is a dream of opposites, indicating that you will be applauded for your good reputation.

Friends—A disturbing dream involving a distant friend in trouble is a sign that they are sick or in some kind of trouble. If your dream is calm and happy, you can expect good news soon.

Frightened—To dream that you are terrified by something is a dream to the contrary. Terror implies bliss; fright, joy; pain, pleasure. Your deals, negotiations, etc. will be successful. If you dream that you overcome your fears, things will take a glorious turn for the better and you will be suddenly prosperous.

Frogs—To dream of frogs is favorable: it indicates success in work and business. To the farmer, a fair season and good crops.

Frost—This dream indicates trouble on the horizon. An unfaithful, cruel lover or unsuccessful business.

Frown—*(See Anger.)*

Fruit—Apples indicate long life and success, faithfulness from your sweetheart, and wealth from your business.

Apricots denote health and prosperity, a quick marriage, kind children, and success in love.

Cherries indicate disappointment in love and frustration in marriage.

Currants predict happiness in life, success in your plans, and fidelity in your sweetheart.

Elderberries augur contentment and wealth; success in business; to the farmer, good crops.

Figs are the forerunners of prosperity, happiness, and good business. They are also indicative of a coming inheritance.

Gooseberries indicate many children, particularly sons, and success in accomplishing your goals. To the sailor they are a sign of danger in their next voyage.

Grapes denote happiness in marriage and success in work.

Hazelnuts forebode conflict and anger from friends; bad business and complete disappointment for the lover.

Lemons denote conflict in the family and anxiety about children; they announce the death of a relative, and disappointment in love.

Melons announce speedy recovery to those who are sick; they indicate harmony, and inform you that you will quickly settle a disagreement.

Mulberries are a good sign; they foretell a quick and happy marriage and are particularly favorable to sailors and farmers.

Oranges are very bad omens; they forebode loss of wealth and reputation, theft, and sickness and injury for your lover.

Peaches are very favorable to the dreamer; if you are in love, they foretell that your love is returned; they indicate wealth, good crops to the farmer, and a successful voyage to the sailor.

Pears indicate sickness; if you gather them up it's a sign of a prosperous business.

Frustrated—To dream you are frustrated and angry indicates you will soon be delighted by good news.

Gala—To dream that you are at a party or gala indicates that you will be well off enough to be able to travel to distant places.

Gallows—It is a dream of opposites. You will be lucky in all ways—success in work, much money, honor, a high position.

Game—To dream that you are playing a game and win is a sign that you will be very successful; but if in your dream you lose, it indicates you will be unlucky.

Game (animal)—If you see game in the woods and shoot it, it is a sign that you will win the heart of the one you love. If the animal is decomposing, it indicates the decay of health and business.

Garden—If you dream of an abundant garden, full of flowers and fruit, it is a very fortunate dream indicating good luck in every sphere of life.

Garter—To dream that you lose your garter indicates that your circumstances in life will be difficult and uncomfortable. If you dream that your lover picks it up and gives it to you, it indicates their sincerity and the strength of their affection.

Gather—To dream of gathering up money is a sign that your income will increase. To gather fruit in season indicates great enjoyment, health, and happiness; but if it is out of season, it is a sign of grief caused by rivals and unfaithful love.

Gem—To dream you wear a costly gem signifies you will not continue to succeed as well as you have. Prepare for difficult days ahead.

Ghost—To dream you see a horrifying ghost is a very bad omen. You will encounter overwhelming difficulties. But if you are brave in your dream and watch the ghost vanish, it indicates that you will overcome your situation.

Gifts—To dream you receive a present is good, and indicates that good fortune is about to visit you, as well as marriage. To dream you have given a gift to someone else indicates sickness.

Glass—To dream that you look through clear glass indicates that you are on the path to success. If the glass is obscured and hard to see through, it indicates that your path is uncertain and you will meet with problems. If you dream you cannot see through the glass at all, your circumstances are fixed and you will not be able to change them.

Gleaning—To dream you are in the harvest field gleaning ears of corn indicates that you will thrive in life through your own work. But if you cannot find any corn, it indicates that your life will be fruitless.

Gloomy—To dream you feel gloomy and depressed is good, signifying the opposite.

Gloves—To dream that you lose your gloves indicates setbacks in work and a loss of business. If you lose only your left glove, then you will move soon; your right glove, then you will lose your partner.

Goats—You will have enemies and face many problems created by the lies of others, but you will be happy in spite of it all. Your setbacks will not sink you, but will work in your favor.

God—This is a rare dream—typically only those who are about to die have it. It is always a token of death. Except if you dream of a conversation with God, which indicates that you will live a life of honor and usefulness.

Gold—"To dream of gold," says Ptolemy, "is a dream on contrary. It is a sign of poverty and distress. Gold is often an omen of sickness and sadness."

Good—To dream that you do something good for anyone signifies pleasure and joy. To dream that others help you indicates profit.

Goodbye—If you dream of bidding your friends or relatives goodbye, prepare for sickness, ill health, and trouble; sadness will soon mark your path.

Goose—This is a bad dream for a single man; the person he loves will prove a very incompetent partner.

Gooseberries—*(See Fruit.)*

Gossip—To dream that you have been the subject of gossip signifies that you will receive the object of your desires. Expect to hear that someone higher up has spoken well of you.

Gown—*(See Clothes or Dress.)*

Grain—To dream that you see grain is a fortunate omen; it implies that through hard work and perseverance you will become wealthy and be well respected. To the farmer it indicates fair seasons and good crops.

Grapes—*(See Fruit.)*

Grass—Green grass is a sign of wealth and continual prosperity; if you dream of withered and decayed grass, the dream is a sign of sickness and sadness.

Grave—To dream of an open grave is a sign that a friend or relative will make devasting choices. If you dream it while severely ill, recovery is unlikely.

Grief—To dream that you are present at the death of a loved one indicates that you will soon marry well; if you're already married, it signifies a new business partnership.

Groans—To dream you hear groaning, as if someone is in pain, signifies that one of your neighbors or friends will mysteriously disappear.

Ground—For a person to dream they fall on the ground indicates dishonor, shame, and grief. Be careful!

Gun—To dream that you hear a gunshot indicates that you will hear of the death of a distant friend or relative; it also portends that you will be slandered by your rivals and is bad luck for people in business.

Gutter—To dream you find something valuable in a gutter is a sign you will soon find money or a piece of jewelry that you will value very much.

Haggard—To dream your face has become haggard and worn indicates good news from far away relatives and friends.

Hail—To dream that it is hailing or snowing is a bad dream. It indicates disappointed hopes and bad luck. To the farmer, it means poor crops and to the businessperson, a loss.

Hair—If you dream that you have beautiful hair it indicates sickness. If you dream that your hair is falling out it indicates bad business or the illness of your partner.

Halter—To dream that you see a halter around the neck of an animal indicates that some of your relatives or friends will rise to positions of power.

Ham—To dream of ham is good. It indicates health and plenty. You will be very happy in your domestic life.

Handcuffs—A bad dream, denoting that if you are not careful you will fall into a life of crime for which you will pay dearly.

Hands—Dreaming that your hands are tied indicates problems that will be difficult to overcome. To dream your hands are dirty means that you are at risk of behaving dishonorably or are about to begin an unsuccessful venture.

Handsome—For anyone to dream they are very handsome signifies that they will soon become sick with a disease that will mar their looks.

Handwriting—To dream you see the handwriting of a dead friend is a warning to consider your own character and choices.

Hanging—To dream that you are being hanged indicates that you will rise in social status and be wealthy. To dream that you see someone hanged is a good omen for that person.

Happy—To dream that you are happy signifies the reverse, denoting something unpleasant will happen.

Hares—To dream you see a hare chased by a dog indicates that your adversaries will work against you, but that you will elude them. To dream you see several hares indicates faithful friends.

Harmony—To dream you hear music or that you listen to a harmony is a sign of a long and happy life. This dream is a good omen for everyone.

Harp—To dream you are playing the harp is a sign that some envious person is trying to injure you by gossiping about you and spreading false rumors.

Harvest—To dream of a harvest is a good sign; you couldn't have had a better dream. It indicates prosperity in whatever profession you find yourself in.

Hat—To dream you have a new hat is a sign of success. To dream you lose your hat, or that it is taken off your head, means you have an enemy who will seek to do you harm both in the open and in secret.

Hate—To dream you hate a person indicates you will always have a good friend in your time of need.

Hawk—If you dream you see a hawk, it signifies you are about to begin a new venture of some kind. If the hawk swoops down and catches its prey, you will succeed. But if a songbird attacks the hawk, you will encounter many difficulties and might not succeed.

Hay—To dream you are cutting hay indicates that you will have great influence in society. To dream of raking it indicates you will be respected by powerful people.

Heart—To dream you have heart disease or experience heart palpitations indicates trouble.

Heat—To dream of being in an extremely hot place indicates anger, and that someone is preparing to scold or argue with you.

Heaven—To dream of heaven indicates a change of worlds. The rest of your life will be spiritually happy, and your death peaceful.

Hedgehog—To dream you see one indicates you will meet an old friend that you haven't seen in years.

Hedges—To dream of green hedges is a sign of good circumstances. If you are blocked by thorny hedges, it indicates that you will suffer at the hand of rivals both in work and in love.

Heir—To dream you are the heir to an inheritance indicates that you will be left out of your relatives' wills. It is not a good dream.

Hell—This dream predicts suffering caused by enemies, bad business, and grief.

Hen—To hear hens cluck in your dream signifies joy, love, and profit at work.

Herbs—Different herbs have different meanings according to their natures and medical uses. Hemlock, henbane, aconite, and any poisonous herb indicates you are in danger. To dream of useful and fragrant herbs is good. Sage indicates honor and advancement. Thyme indicates a happy marriage and prosperity. Balm indicates sickness, but a speedy recovery. Wormwood, bitter trials.

Hills—To dream of climbing a high hill and being unable to reach the top is a sign that you will have to work hard all your life, but will never be wealthy. If you reach the top, it shows great success.

Hoe—To dream you see this tool signifies you will enjoy good health for some time.

Hogs—*(See Pigs.)*

Home—To dream of your childhood home indicates health and prosperity. To the lover it signifies mutual love and a happy marriage.

Homeless—To dream you are without a home is a good omen; it indicates that you will receive a large sum of money, and is generally the precursor to good luck.

Homicide—To dream of committing homicide indicates great sadness and loss in your life.

Honey—To dream you are eating honey indicates good health, long life, success in business, and great enjoyment.

Hops—To dream you see a garden full of hops, in full leaf, signifies wealth and abundance; if you see dried hops, and smell their fragrance, it indicates you will soon receive an inheritance.

Horn—To dream you hear the sound of a horn indicates you will hear news from a friend in a distant country. To hear the sound repeatedly indicates coming conflict and disagreements.

Horse—Dreaming of this noble animal is generally good. To dream that you are riding a beautiful horse is a sign of future independence and happiness. But if it throws you, it indicates that your goals will be unmet.

Horseshoe—To see a horseshoe in your dream denotes good fortune in your work and home. To dream you find a horseshoe signifies you will win the lottery.

Hospital—To dream you visit a hospital indicates you will have health, strength, peace, and happiness in your home life.

Hounds—To dream of chasing a pack of hounds indicates that your ambitions will not be very successful and your lover will disappoint you.

House—To dream you build a house foretells great prosperity at work. If a sailor dreams of building a house, it foretells a successful voyage.

Hug—To dream you are hugging your relatives is a warning of lies and disloyalty; if friends, disappointment; if you hug a person you do not know, you will travel.

Hummingbirds—This dream indicates travel to a foreign country and that you will find great success in work there.

Hunger—To dream that you are very hungry indicates that you will come up in the world through your own intelligence and work.

Hunting—To dream that you hunt anything, and capture it, is a good sign of worldly prosperity; but, if you lose it, it indicates the opposite.

Hurricane—This dream indicates danger to the traveler and sailor, and disappointment for lovers. It is a bad sign for the businessperson and a warning of family fighting.

Hurt—To dream that you have hurt yourself, or that someone has hurt you, is a dream to the contrary, and implies that you will succeed, whether in work or in love.

Husband—To dream you have one is a dream of opposites; you will not marry.

Hymns—*(See Singing.)*

Ice—Dreaming of ice is always bad. It foretells failure at work and unsuccessful ventures. To the sailor it indicates disasters; to the farmer, destroyed crops.

Icicles—To dream you see icicles suspended is a sign of good luck.

Idiot—This is a dream of opposites. To dream you behave like an idiot foretells that you will be competent in your various endeavors.

Idle—To dream that you are lazy indicates profit and growth, both mentally and in your bank account; you will climb the ladder through hard work and perseverance.

Ill—To dream that you are sick indicates that you are in danger of succumbing to temptation.

Illness—*(See Sickness.)*

Illumination—Dreaming of sudden illumination indicates a joyful occasion has arrived. You will be happy in love and travel. This is a happy dream, and it is always followed by good things.

Image—To dream you see an image or statue signifies beloved children in your life.

Imprisonment—It is a dream to the contrary. It is a sign of liberty in every sense and enjoyment, especially in a relationship.

Imps—This dream betokens great grief and vexation. People around you will frustrate you endlessly. It indicates you are dealing with malicious people.

Income—For a person to dream their income is not enough to meet their cost of living indicates they will be able to save money; but if they dream they have money left after paying their bills, it is a sign that they will always be poor.

Increase—To dream you have an increase of good things in your life is an unfortunate dream, denoting scarcity of spending money, clothing, and the necessities of life.

Independence—If you dream you earn enough money to retire early and leave your work, you can be certain that though you might make money you will lose it, which will prevent you from retiring.

Indifference—If in your dream you feel indifferent, it indicates your affairs will continue on as usual in every way.

Industry—To dream you are busy at work indicates health and prosperity, and a rise in your social standing.

Infirm—To dream you are infirm indicates health for yourself and your children. To dream of someone else who is infirm signals sickness or sadness.

Infirmary—To dream you are in an infirmary indicates an accident or sickness. To dream you leave it is a sign of recovery.

Influence—To dream that you rise to a position of influence in the place where you live is a sign that your good intentions will be misunderstood; you will encounter many obstacles, both in business and religion.

Inheritance—To dream you have an inheritance indicates disappointment, financial loss, and poverty.

Injury—To dream that someone has injured you indicates

that you have enemies. To the farmer it predicts a poor season of crops.

Ink—To dream you are writing with ink indicates prosperity in work; if the ink spills or you get it on your hands, your message will not be successful, whether they are business letters or love notes.

Inn—To dream of staying at an inn indicates poverty and failure in your undertakings; it is the forerunner of sickness, and sometimes death.

Insane—To dream you are insane indicates good health, domestic happiness, and long life.

Insult—To dream that you are insulted indicates trouble and frustration caused by someone who owes you money; it is always the forerunner of irritation.

Intemperance—To dream of being excessive in eating or drinking foretells sickness and trouble.

Invite—To dream you are invited to a party or other event indicates that your expectations will be disappointed.

Iron—To dream you are injured by an iron signifies that your plans will go amiss or you will be physically injured.

Itch—To dream of having an itch indicates difficulty and trouble in both love and business.

Ivory—This dream portends abundance for the farmer, success in business, and a safe voyage to the sailor.

Ivy—To dream of ivy is a sign that your friend, lover, or partner will cling to you the way ivy does to a wall; you will have good health and a long, prosperous life.

Jackdaw—To dream that one crosses your path is a sign of bitter rivals who will try to do you harm. To dream that you catch the jackdaw indicates that you will overcome these rivals.

Jail—To dream you are in jail is very favorable. Your good reputation will grow after this dream.

Jailor—To dream of a jailor indicates that some of your friends who have been in prison will soon be free.

Jar—To see a jar full of anything is good for business; but if it is empty, expect that you will work in vain.

Jaundice—To dream you have jaundice indicates sickness, poverty, or conflict is at hand. To dream that your partner has jaundice is a sign that they are unfaithful.

Jealousy—To dream that you are jealous of your husband, or wife, or sweetheart, is indicative of trouble and great anxiety. At work, you can expect your affairs to be interrupted by unforeseen factors.

Jewels—It is always a good dream; a harbinger of great prosperity. To dream your lover gives you jewels is a sign that their affection is real, and you will certainly marry.

Jolly—If you dream you are in good company and feel particularly happy and jolly, it signifies sorrow. Remember who made you laugh and be careful of them as they might be the cause of your coming sorrow.

Journey—To dream that you have to go on a journey to a distant country predicts a major change in your life. If the journey is enjoyable, the change will be positive. If not, the change will also be difficult.

Judge—To dream you stand before a judge indicates that you will be involved in a dispute, or have serious charges made against you. It is a dream of opposites. If the judge acquits you, you will be found guilty. If he condemns you, you will be successful and will emerge from the ordeal unharmed.

Jug—To dream you drink out of a jug indicates a coming trip. If the jug is large, it will be a long journey; if small, a short journey. If the liquid inside is good, the journey will be as well. If it's unpleasant, the journey will be full of trouble.

Jumping—To dream that you are jumping signals that you will meet with obstacles and setbacks, but that you will overcome them.

Juniper—To dream of juniper is unlucky, especially if the dreamer is ill; but to dream of gathering juniper berries foretells prosperity and joy.

Kernel—*(See Nuts.)*

Kettle—To dream you see a bright copper kettle indicates joy and peace in domestic and everyday life.

Key—To dream you lose a key indicates disappointment and displeasure; to dream you give someone a key indicates a marriage; to dream of many keys indicates riches.

King—To dream you speak to a king indicates that you will rise in social status; but if the monarch is unfriendly, your expectations will be disappointed.

Kiss—To dream of kissing someone you should not is a bad sign; it indicates a false friend, or a false lover. To see another kiss your intended predicts that you will have a rival. To see your lover kiss another person indicates false love from a false heart. For married people to dream of kissing each other is a sign that they will meet an unfaithful companion.

Kite—To dream you see a kite flying high indicates that your status will rise. If you are flying it yourself and if it flies high and steady, it's a good sign. But if the string breaks, and the kite is blown away, it is a very bad dream.

Kitten—To dream you are playing with a kitten and it scratches you indicates that if you marry you will have a very unhappy life.

Knee—To dream you are wounded in the knee is a sign you will be unhappy and discontent due to envy; a dream of a swollen knee means grief, sickness, or trouble. Anything relating to the knee is unfortunate.

Knife—This is a very unfavorable dream. If you see dinner knives cleaned and ready for a meal, it is a sign of coming poverty. If you see a bright, sharp knife it indicates that you have enemies or rivals.

Labor—To dream you are laboring and working hard indicates that you will have an easy life. To dream that you watch others work indicates that you will gain wealth through manufacturing.

Ladder—If you are young and dream that you have reached the top of the ladder, good things are ahead of you and you will achieve your goals. If you are in business it is a sign of wealth and recognition. But if you dream you reach the top of the ladder and feel dizzy when you look down, it means that you will not be able to maintain your new status. If you dream the ladder breaks as you climb, it means you will never reach your goals.

Lake—To dream of sailing on a glassy lake indicates that you will be fortunate. But if the lake is muddy or rough, it predicts that you will experience obstacles and trouble.

Lambs—It is always good to dream about a lamb. If you have children it indicates that they will be well and flourish.

Lame—To dream you are lame implies that your life will include many obstacles and difficulties.

Lament—To dream you are lamenting a loss—whether grief from the death of someone you love or a painful loss at work or in love—is a dream of opposites; you will soon have cause to celebrate.

Lamps—If you dream you are carrying a bright lamp, it predicts that you will succeed in your work and become well-respected. It's a good omen for a lover. If you dream that you carry a lamp that is dim, it is a sign of sickness. If the light goes out as you carry it, it foretells your death or that your plans and ambitions will not be successful.

Land—To dream that you own land indicates wealth and independence. To dream that you have sold your property indicates that you will soon move, probably to a foreign country.

Lantern—To dream of carrying a lantern in a dark night is a good sign; it indicates that you will achieve your hopes. If you stumble, it indicates trouble.

Lark—It is very lucky to dream you hear a lark singing; it indicates health and prosperity.

Laughing—To dream that you are laughing loudly indicates coming disappointment. If you are in love it is a certain sign that your love will not be reciprocated. Laughter is often a sign of tears and sadness.

Laurel—To dream about a laurel is a sign of victory and pleasure. If you marry, it foretells that your spouse will be wealthy.

Law—If you dream that you are involved in a lawsuit, it is a sign of loss and difficulty in your business and work. After this dream it would be very risky to enter into any new partnership, contract, or business agreement.

Lawyer—To dream you meet a lawyer indicates that you will receive bad news; if you speak to them, you will discover you have lost some property or possession; if you hear someone talking about the lawyer you will experience some misfortune.

Lead—To dream of lead indicates troubles and quarrels. For the sailor, it is a sign of shipwreck and narrow escape from drowning.

Leaping—If you dream of leaping over any object it indicates you will overcome every obstacle and will grow to become well-respected for your work.

Learning—To dream of being in a place of learning shows

that you will be respected for your hard work. It's a good sign to dream that you are learning something new and will master it quickly and easily.

Leather—To dream you see a large amount of leather indicates that your work will be reliable, but boring.

Leaves—If you see the trees covered with beautiful green leaves it is good. You will succeed at work. If you dream you see blossoms, and then fruit among the leaves, it indicates that you will marry. If the leaves are brown and dried, it portends trouble or loss at work and a season of bad crops for the farmer.

Ledger—If you dream of misplacing a ledger, be careful of your accountant or bookkeeper as they may be stealing from you.

Leech—To dream you see a leech is a sign of sickness. If you dream that one bites you, you will be seriously injured by someone.

Lemons—To dream that you are eating a lemon indicates a coming illness. To dream you see a large number of lemons indicates that your marriage will become disappointing and bitter.

Lending—Not a good dream. You will be surrounded by needy dependents who will be at best irritating, and at worst will cause you financial problems.

Leopard—To dream of these beautiful, fierce creatures indicates that you will travel to a new country and will encounter trouble there.

Leprosy—To dream that you have leprosy is always the forerunner of trouble and misfortunes. It may imply that you have been guilty of some crime that leads to disgrace and likely imprisonment.

Letter—Dreaming of receiving a letter sometimes indicates that you will receive a gift or unexpected news from a person you have not heard from for many years. To dream that you send a letter indicates you will soon be able to perform a generous act.

Lettuce—To dream that you eat lettuce indicates trouble and struggle.

Lice—This dream foretells sickness, poverty, and struggle. You or someone you love will meet with significant trials.

Lifeboat—To dream you are saved by a lifeboat shows success in your affairs; to dream you simply see a lifeboat is not important.

Light—To dream you see a brilliant light indicates wealth and prestige. If you see it suddenly extinguished, it indicates that your plans will not come to fruition.

Lighthouse—If you dream you see a lighthouse, it indicates danger in your pathway; you will make a wreck of yourself by making bad choices.

Lightning—It is a favorable dream, for it predicts success in business and that you will earn a good reputation. To the farmer it is a sign of a good season of crops and of safe, successful voyages for the sailor.

Lily—To dream you see this lovely flower is a sign that you will be happy and prosperous in your career by virtue of your hard work.

Linen—To dream that you are dressed in clean white linen indicates that you will soon receive good news. It's a sign of success in work and domestic happiness. If the linen is dirty, the meaning is reversed and it is a sign of lack and difficulty.

Lion—This dream indicates greatness and future prestige. You will occupy a powerful and important position.

Lips—To dream your friends have full, lovely lips indicates they will have good health; but if they look dry and chapped the reverse is true.

Liquors—To dream that you drink brandy is a certain sign that you will have a prosperous life in a foreign country. If you dream that you drink rum, it is a sign that your partner will work in shipping or transportation. If you dream that you drink gin, it foretells that you will live in a city, experience financial hardship, and behave dishonorably. Dreaming of drinking whiskey predicts that you will suddenly lose your wealth and friends.

Lizard—To dream you see a lizard is not a good sign, denoting bad luck and misfortune caused by secret enemies.

Load—To dream that you are carrying a heavy load foretells that your future life will be one of hard work. But if in your dream you are able to carry your load, then it is a sign that you will be able to rise above all your difficulties.

Loaves—If you dream you see a large number of loaves of bread, it means you will experience want and need.

Lobsters—To dream of eating lobsters foretells trouble and sorrows.

Lock—To dream about a lock implies that your success will be hindered by obstacles. If you see doors, cabinets, drawers, etc. with locks and no keys, it is a bad sign for lovers and those in business. If you dream you find a key that opens the locks, the meaning shifts. You will succeed, you will acquire, and you will rise.

Loom—To dream you are busy weaving indicates you will be industrious and thrifty, and know your business.

Love—To dream you do not find love is a dream to the contrary; you will find love and be happy. To dream that friends love you foretells success at work and domestic happiness. To dream of spending time with your lover means that you will soon marry them or, if you are pregnant, that you will have a healthy baby. To dream of loving and being loved indicates that you will enjoy a large circle of loyal, loving friends who will be ready to help you no matter what.

Lovely—For a person to dream they see a lovely young woman indicates they will marry a cheerful person. If you look lovely in your dream expect sickness.

Lucky—To dream that you are lucky is a dream of opposites. You will experience bad luck.

Luggage—To dream that you are traveling and carrying heavy bags is a sign that you will experience frustrations and setbacks.

Lumber—To dream that you are surrounded by lumber foretells trouble. To dream that you find something valuable in the wood is a sign that you will earn or inherit a fortune.

Luxury—Dreaming of living in great luxury is a sign of sickness and coming disappointments.

Lying—If you dream you are telling a lie, that is not a good sign.

Lynx—To dream of a lynx is an unfortunate dream—it indicates that there are enemies or rivals who mean you harm.

Mad dog—To dream you meet a mad dog is a good dream. You will be fortunate in everything you undertake, and your efforts will meet with success.

Madness—To dream you are mad, or are in the company of someone who is, indicates that you are intelligent and will devote yourself to profitable work. You will be healthy and wealthy and enjoy a long life.

Magic—Dreaming of magic foretells change and revolution. Your circumstances will change for the better. It can also indicate that a trusted friend will be revealed to be a liar but that you will emerge unscathed.

Magnet—To dream that you see a number of magnets foretells that your path will be filled with distractions and temptations that will not serve you. If you dream that you are holding or using a magnet, it indicates that you are manipulating someone for selfish purposes.

Magpie—To dream that you see a magpie foretells that you will soon be married, but that you will lose your partner a few years after your marriage.

Malice—To dream that someone bears you malice is a sign of good luck in your affairs; you will rise in the world either through hard work or by your marriage.

Malt—To dream that you are brewing malt into beer is a sign of marriage. To dream that you see a quantity of malt is an omen of prosperity, long life, and a comfortable old age.

Mansion—If you dream you are living in a mansion that is a bad sign. It means that you or one of your friends will have an accident.

Manslaughter—To dream you have been guilty of manslaughter foretells misunderstandings, conflict, and family fights. You will disagree with a close friend.

Map—If you dream that you are reading a map it is a sign that you will move to a foreign country for many years before eventually returning home.

Marigolds—Dreaming of marigolds promises a constant lover, a happy marriage, and a rise in social standing.

Market—To dream that you are visiting or selling at a market indicates success in business. It is also a sign of a coming celebration.

Marmalade—To dream you are eating marmalade alone is a

sign of coming sickness. To dream you are eating it with someone else indicates you will meet a kind friend who is ready to cheer you up.

Marriage—Dreaming you are married is a sign of death. It is very unfavorable for the dreamer; it indicates poverty, prison, misfortune, and the loss of love. To dream you attend or assist at a wedding is a sign of good news and that you will advance in life.

Mars—To dream of Mars, the god of war, is unfortunate; expect fighting among friends and family. You will be unhappy in your marriage.

Marsh—To dream that you are walking in marshy country indicates a troubled life. If you can hardly walk because of the wet ground, it indicates sadness and difficulties. But if you escape the marsh, it is a sign that you will overcome your situation and find happiness.

Mat—For a person to dream their doormat has been stolen indicates that someone will try to break into their house.

Meadow—To dream that you are walking through a meadow predicts good fortune and happiness.

Measles—To dream that you are sick with the measles indicates that you will enjoy a sudden, unexpected windfall.

Meat—For a person to dream they see meat indicates loss and damage. If you eat it, it is a sign of sickness.

Medals—To dream of medals awarded for good conduct shows a loss of character and lack of honor.

Medicine—If you dream you are taking awful-tasting medicine, it implies that something unpleasant will happen for a short time, but that in the long run it will prove to be very useful.

Melancholy—To dream that you feel depressed and sad is a sign that you will soon hear some very good news.

Merry—To dream you are merry and joyful indicates trouble and strong feelings of sadness, possibly sickness.

Mice—To dream of mice indicates that rivals, gossips, and enemies are meddling in your life. It can also entail poverty and unsuccessful undertakings.

Milk—To dream that you are drinking milk foretells joy. To dream of selling milk indicates bad business and disappointments in love. To dream that you give milk to someone indicates prosperity and a happy marriage. Milking a cow foretells success for a farmer and abundant crops.

Mime—To dream that you watch a mime implies that you live with deceitful people.

Mine—To dream that you descend into a coal mine shows success in trade; but if you get hurt, expect losses and disappointments.

Minister—*(See Clergyman.)*

Mirror—For a person to dream that they stand in front of a mirror indicates that they will lose their looks and their character will be tainted by scandal.

Miser—This is an unlucky dream. It foretells a lack of success and trouble. You will not advance above your current circumstances, but will likely become poorer.

Miserable—To dream that you are miserable indicates that some unexpected good fortune is coming your way.

Misfortune—To dream that something unfortunate has happened to you or to your partner means exactly the contrary. It indicates that you will be successful in work and enjoy a happy relationship.

Mist—To dream you are enveloped in a thick mist indicates that your ambitions will succeed, even if things look dark right now.

Moles—To dream of having moles on any part of your body signifies good health.

Money—To dream that you purchase something with money indicates that you will be successful in business. To dream that you receive money foretells the birth of a child or that you will win a lawsuit. To dream you find money foretells sudden advancement through success at work or through marriage.

Monkeys—To dream you see a large number of monkeys indicates you will suffer from mischief caused by someone you used to trust.

Moon—To dream of the moon foretells unexpected joy and success in love. The new moon is a good sign for businesspeople, farmers, and lovers. The full moon indicates marriage.

Mother—To dream that you see your mother and have a warm conversation with her indicates comfort and prosperity through life.

Moths—To dream of moths indicates enemies who are working against you. It also indicates a fight between you and your lover and probably a coming separation.

Mountain—To dream you are ascending a steep, tall mountain indicates a life of hard work, toil, and sorrow; but, if you reach the top, you will overcome all difficulties.

Mourning—This is a dream of opposites. It is a sign of good things to come. To the married, it indicates happiness and contentment, wealth to the businessman, and success to the sailor and farmer.

Mouse—*(See Mice).*

Murder—To dream you have committed murder is a terrible dream. It foretells that you will behave viciously and will probably end up in prison. After this dream you need to change your life or the repercussions will be serious and violent.

Mushrooms—To dream that you are eating mushrooms indicates personal sickness. To dream that you are gathering them foretells wealth.

Music—To dream you hear beautiful music indicates joyful news from a long absent friend. Unpleasant and discordant music indicates trouble and vexation.

Mute—Dreaming of being unable to speak indicates that you will embarrass or shame yourself so deeply you will be unable to defend your actions.

Need—To dream you find yourself in need of money signifies that you will become wealthy and prosperous.

Nervous—*(See Afraid.)*

Nest—Dreaming of a bird's nest indicates marriage and domestic happiness or good business. If you dream of a bird's nest with broken eggs, or dead birds, it is a sign of failure and distress.

Nettles—To dream of nettles is a symbol of good health and prosperity. If you dream you are stung by nettles, it indicates frustration and disappointment.

News—To dream you hear some strange news indicates that your lover or partner is going to encounter serious trouble.

Night—To dream that day suddenly becomes night indicates that your life will suddenly take a turn for the worse. To dream that you are walking on a dark night indicates grief and disappointment and loss. If you are in business, you will make poor business decisions and end up in debt.

Nightingale—To dream of hearing this sweet-singing bird is a very good omen; it is always the harbinger of joy, success, and prosperity. It's a good dream for people experiencing adversity or illness as it signals that these circumstances will change.

Nightmare—To dream that you have a nightmare signifies that you are being controlled by a bad and harmful habit.

Nobility—For a person to dream they are a noble or aristocrat signifies that trouble is about to visit them and their social standing will fall.

Noises—To dream of hearing a loud, alarming noise foretells fighting and squabbling at home.

Nose—To dream one has a lovely nose is good and indicates wealth and prosperity. You will also make the acquaintance of a rich person.

Nosebleed—To dream that your nose is bleeding indicates that you will get sick and your life will be in danger. To people in business, it indicates heavy losses. If engaged in a trial or lawsuit, it signals that you will be almost overwhelmed by legal fees.

Nursing—To dream you are nursing a baby means that you will soon be given a very important role or task and will be rewarded generously for your work.

Nuts—To dream of nuts is a sign of prosperity, denoting that you will become wealthy through a generous inheritance.

Oak—To dream of a large oak, with beautiful foliage, is a very good dream. To someone in business, it indicates a steady, reliable trade, and that they will be able to endure and overcome all obstacles. To a family it indicates constant and abiding happiness. It also forebodes a happy and healthy old age. To dream of an oak full of acorns foretells unbounded prosperity. To dream of a withered oak indicates that your dearest hopes will not amount to anything, and you will experience poverty in your later years. A blasted oak foretells sudden death.

Oar—If you dream you lose one of your oars while on a boat it indicates the death of your father, mother, or someone to whom you look for protection.

Oats—For a farmer to dream that he sees oats in the field or elsewhere indicates a bountiful harvest, and a good reaping. For a businessperson it predicts good business and prosperity. To those starting a new venture it is a sign of coming success.

Ocean—To dream that you are looking at the ocean when it is calm is good; when it is stormy, it predicts trouble. To dream of sailing on the ocean when it is smooth indicates the accomplishment of a goal or plan, as well as success in love.

Offense—To dream that someone has offended you is a sign that you will have a fight or quarrel with your lover or close friend. You will stop talking for some time. If you dream that you are so offended you seek revenge, or vice versa, it is a dangerous sign.

Office—To dream you lose your role in an office or as an elected official foreshows death and loss of property. To the lover it means your sweetheart does not love you and that your marriage would be unhappy.

Oil—To dream you are anointed with oil is a good omen.

Olives—To dream you are gathering olives indicates peace, delight, and happiness in any situation. To dream you are eating olives foretells you will rise above your present circumstances, regardless of what they are.

Onions—To dream you are eating onions predicts that you will find valuable treasure. To dream you are cutting onions and crying indicates squabbles with your friends or family.

Oranges—*(See Fruit.)*

Orchard—To dream that you are in an orchard gathering good fruit indicates that you will be the heir to a fortune and become wealthy. If the fruit is ripe, this will happen soon; if it is still unripe it will not happen for some time.

Organ—To dream that you hear an organ being played predicts great prosperity and success in your work.

Ornaments—To dream you see or buy ornaments indicates that you will suffer financially due to overspending.

Orphans—Whoever dreams of an orphan will receive money from a stranger. Dreaming about orphans is always good.

Oven—To dream you are baking something in an oven predicts moderate success in trade. But if you burn the bread, it portends disaster; your business will fail, and for a season you will experience poverty.

Overboard—To dream that you have fallen overboard indicates sickness, poverty, imprisonment, and failure in your undertakings.

Owl—To dream you see this bird and hear it hoot indicates sickness, poverty, and disgrace.

Ox—To dream that you see a herd of oxen is a sign of success in your endeavors, particularly if you see them grazing, which indicates great wealth or a rise in social class.

Oysters—To dream of eating oysters foretells that after conflict and loss you will acquire wealth; for married people it means happiness, and for lovers it means they will win the heart of the one they love.

Package—To dream that you receive a package is a sign of good fortune. You will either hear from a friend or receive a present.

Pain—This is a dream of opposites. To dream that you suffer great pain indicates that you will soon benefit tremendously, whether in work, life, or love.

Painting—To dream you paint your house indicates sickness in the family, but at the same time thrift and good luck in business. If in your dream you see a freshly painted white house, it is a sign of a coming funeral. Dreaming of beautiful paintings and landscapes indicates poverty and bad luck.

Palace—To dream that you live in a palace is a good omen, foreshadowing wealth and a good reputation. To the lover it predicts a kind partner, and a happy marriage.

Pall—For a young person to dream they see a pall, or velvet covering, under which a corpse is borne to the grave, indicates they will soon be married.

Pancakes—To dream that you are eating pancakes indicates that something for which you have long been waiting and anticipating will soon happen.

Paper—To dream of paper implies that you will get into trouble and be accused of crimes that will cost a great deal of money and anxiety before you can prove yourself innocent.

Paradise—This is a good dream, promising married people a happy, content life, and sure entrance into Paradise.

It's a good omen for farmers, emigrants, and people in business.

Parents—If your parents are dead and you dream that they visit you, this is a warning to be very careful in new business deals and ventures. If you have been living carelessly, their visit was to rebuke you and warn you of danger.

Park—To dream of walking through a park indicates health and happiness. If you dream that you are walking with another person, it indicates a faithful lover and a quick marriage.

Parting—To dream of parting from friends with regret indicates that you will experience disappointment; for lovers, it means jealousy.

Partnership—If you dream of entering a new business partnership, it's a sign that it would be better to hold off for a time as you will be more successful by yourself.

Partridge—If you dream that you see a flock of partridges it is a sign of misfortune, but if they fly away, it means you will overcome the situation and be happy.

Party—*(See Ball.)*

Passion—*(See Anger.)*

Patches—If you dream of patching clothes it is an excellent dream that will bring you riches.

Path—Walking a good path indicates success at work and in matters of love. If the path appears crooked and thorny in your dream, it foretells disappointments and treacherous friends.

Pawnbroker—To dream of pawning something foretells losses and disappointment. You will have some quarrel that will end in a trial or lawsuit that you will lose and will almost ruin you.

Peaches—To dream you are eating peaches foretells a short-lived sickness.

Peacock—To dream that you see a peacock with its feathers spread indicates an uncertain position in life.

Pearls—This is a very favorable dream; it foretells that you, regardless of your current situation, will die a wealthy, contented person, well-loved and respected.

Pears—*(See Fruit.)*

Peas—This is a good dream. To dream that you are eating peas indicates great prosperity. If you dream that you see them growing, it foretells good fortune in love and a happy marriage.

Penny—To dream that you are not worth a penny, or that someone gives you a penny, is an evil dream. It signifies a fall in social standing.

Pension—To dream that you have a pension indicates that you will have to listen to a great deal of offensive language and comments.

Perjury—To dream that you have been guilty of perjury foretells that you will make a bad decision that will harm your reputation.

Phantom—*(See Ghost.)*

Pheasants—To dream that you see pheasants flying across

your path or in a field foretells that a relative or friend will leave you an inheritance. If you dream that you see them fight and fly away, you will be in danger of losing your inheritance through a lawsuit.

Pictures—To dream of a picture of a painting is not good; it indicates deceit and lies. No matter how lovely the picture is, it still foretells trouble from a liar who will try to damage your reputation.

Pier—To dream you are standing at the pier in a coastal town and watching the ships come and go indicates you will shortly receive some news, and that your work or business will be successful.

Pigeons—To dream of seeing pigeons flying in the air is a sign that you will receive important news; they also denote a kind and loving partner, and happiness in love.

Pigs—Dreaming about pigs brings a mixture of good and bad luck. You will have many false friends, but will also have a sincere and faithful lover. It implies much sorrow, sickness, and the risk of death, but you will escape with only a slight injury.

Pimples—If you dream that you have broken out in pimples it means that you will be admired for your beauty.

Pineapples—To dream of pineapples is a sign that you will receive an invitation to a wedding or celebration. It also foretells great success in business and work. To the emigrant it is a sign of safe travels and happiness in the country where they settle.

Pirate—To dream you are captured by pirates indicates you will travel into foreign countries and make a fortune.

Pistol—To dream you hear a pistol shot foretells disaster. If you dream you are firing a pistol, it foretells you will marry a passionate, industrious person.

Pit—To dream that you are climbing down into a pit shows that your business is rapidly declining, and that you will experience financial difficulties. To dream of falling into a pit forebodes loss and trouble.

Plague—If one dreams he has the plague, it signifies health and success in business.

Play—To dream that you are watching a play and enjoying it is a sign of happiness in marriage and success in trade. To dream you are performing in a play is not good.

Plough—To dream of a plough is good for business and work, denoting steady gain and increased profit.

Ploughing—If you dream you are ploughing a field, it means you will become wealthy through your own work and effort.

Plums—If you dream you are gathering green plums it foretells sickness in your family. If you dream that you are gathering ripe plums it's a good dream for all. If you dream you pick them up off the ground, and they are rotten, it indicates false friends, a deceitful lover, and that you will experience poverty and social rejection.

Poison—To dream that you ingested poison foretells that your life will take a turn for the worse; it indicates that your business or work will suffer and that people in your life will be dishonest. If you dream you recover from the effects of the poison, it is a sign you will extricate yourself from these problems and do well.

Police—If an innocent person dreams of being arrested by police officers, it indicates that they will receive some sort of honor or recognition. If you dream your partner has been arrested, you will soon learn they have been promoted or recognized in some way.

Poor—To dream of poverty is good; but if you dream you find yourself begging, it indicates that someone will hurt your feelings or insult you, though your luck will still be good.

Pork—For a person to dream they are eating pork indicates sickness and misfortune.

Potatoes—To dream you are digging up potatoes and find many of them indicates good luck; but if you dig up only a few or they're rotten, it indicates bad luck.

Precipice—To dream that you are on the edge of a cliff or precipice is a dream to forewarn you that your current goals and aims will lead to failure and loss.

Primroses—To dream of primroses indicates sickness, deceit, sorrow, and grief.

Prison—To dream that you are in prison is a dream of opposites. It indicates freedom, happiness, and success at work and in business. To dream that you are putting someone in prison foretells that you will be invited to the wedding of an acquaintance or relative.

Profits—For a businessperson to dream that their profits are much larger than usual is a warning of coming trouble and possibly bankruptcy.

Promotion—If you dream that you are promoted at work, it is a sign of success. If you are currently engaged in a lawsuit, or any dispute, it is a sign you will win.

Provisions—To dream that you are hungry and without food or provisions foretells poverty and need. But if you dream you have a stockpile of provisions and supplies for the future, it implies that you will be well provided for in the future.

Pub—To dream that you own or work at a pub indicates that you will be forced to take extreme actions or to act against your own nature. To dream that you are drinking at a pub is a bad omen, indicating sickness, poverty, and debt.

Public office—To dream you lose your role in public office or as an elected official foreshows death and loss of property. To the lover it means your sweetheart does not love you and that your marriage would be unhappy.

Purse—If you dream that you find a purse with money inside, it foreshadows great happiness, particularly in love. To dream of losing a purse foretells sickness.

Quails—It is an unlucky dream, denoting bad news and family fighting.

Quacking—To dream you hear the quacking of ducks indicates you will never possess any money or property.

Quarrels—This is a dream of opposites; if you dream that you are fighting with someone, it foretells success in business or in love.

Quarry—To dream you fall into a quarry indicates sudden bad news, often the sudden death of a friend or family member.

Queen—To dream that you are in the presence of the Queen means that you will rise in social status through your own efforts. You will also have many friends.

Quicksand—To dream that you are walking through quicksand implies that you are surrounded by temptations and dangerous impulses that you aren't even aware of.

Quilt—For a person to dream their quilt is torn indicates that someone they love will become ill.

Rabbits—To dream that you see rabbits foretells that you will flourish in your work or business. It can also mean that children are in your future.

Race—To dream that you run in a race and win indicates that you will be successful in business.

Raffle—This dream of chance foretells that dangerous habits, poor choices, and bad friends will harm you in life.

Raft—To dream of sailing on a raft signifies that you will be successful in travel; but if the raft sinks it is a sign of loss and discredit.

Rage—*(See Anger.)*

Rags—To dream you are dressed in rags is favorable, promising gain and success.

Railway—To dream you are traveling by train is a sign that a friend you haven't seen in years will soon visit.

Rain—To dream of heavy rain generally foretells trouble.

Rainbow—This is a good sign. It signals change, but a change for the better.

Raking—To dream you are raking indicates success in work and prosperity.

Rats—Dreaming of rats is a sign that you will have many rivals and enemies who will cause you trouble and anxiety. If you kill the rats, it is a good sign.

Ravens—This is a bad dream. It declares that trouble is coming and mischief is brewing. You will suffer injustice, contend with poverty and adversity, and have many sorrows.

Reapers—To dream you see the reapers at work in a field indicates prosperity and success in your business or work. If the fields are bare or empty, it indicates that business will be bad.

Reptile—To dream of any sort of reptile is a sign of anger and conflict. If you dream you are bitten, it shows you will suffer injury.

Rescue—To dream you rescue anyone from danger is a sign that you will rise in the world. To dream you've been rescued from drowning indicates you will go into a successful field of work.

Revenge—To dream you are taking revenge against someone indicates that you will experience hardship and trouble.

Rhubarb—If a person dreams they are eating or see rhubarb, it means they will find favor with someone who previously ignored or disliked them.

Rice—To dream of eating rice signifies abundance.

Rich—To dream that you are rich is a dream to the contrary. You will be poor for a long time and will only become well off at the end of your life.

Ring—If you dream that your wedding ring breaks it foreshadows the death of your spouse. If you dream the ring is causing you pain or pressing on your finger it warns that your spouse or someone in your family will become ill. If you dream that someone you love puts a ring on your finger, you will be married.

River—To dream that you see a wide, muddy river that is running quickly indicates trouble in love and work; but if the river is calm, with a glassy surface, it foretells great happiness in love and commercial prosperity.

Rooster—Whoever dreams of hearing a rooster crow must be cautious of some false friend; don't trust the people around you.

Ropes—To dream you are tied with ropes is a warning to be careful in your work and to avoid entering into contracts or legal agreements with others.

Roses—To dream of roses is an omen of happiness, prosperity, and long life. If the roses are dead it indicates trouble and poverty.

Rowing—To dream of rowing a boat indicates success in love and business; if the boat flips over, it's bad.

Running—To dream you are running is a very excellent dream and foretells that you will advance in life. You will take a long journey, which will prove advantageous. But if you fall, be careful as that is a warning of coming misfortune.

Rust—To dream of rust is a bad omen; rusty knives or tools of any kind indicate the destruction of property; rusty nails or utensils are a sign of poverty and trouble.

Sailing—To dream that you are sailing in a ship on smooth water foretells prosperity; on a stormy sea, misfortunes. To dream that you are sailing in a small boat and dock in a harbor is a sign that you will quickly make a fortune.

Sailing ship—To dream you see a sailing ship coming towards you indicates the joyful return of friends; if you see it sail away from you be careful, as that is a warning that you may lose friends.

Sailor—To dream that you are a mariner or sailor is a sign that you will likely immigrate to a new country. If you dream you see a group of sailors, it suggests that you will receive news from abroad or that your business deals will be successful.

Satan—*(See Devil.)*

Scaffold—To dream of climbing up a high scaffold signifies that you will rise in the world. But if you fall, it indicates a misfortune and a loss of income.

Scallops—To dream you are eating scallops indicates sickness and conflict among your relatives.

School—To dream that you are the principal of a school indicates that you will be reduced in your circumstances.

Scissors—To dream of a pair of scissors is a sign of an upcoming marriage.

Scratched—If you are in debt and you dream of being scratched it's a sign that you will pay back what you owe. For others, the dream is a sign of accident, loss, and misfortune.

Sea—To dream of a rough sea predicts trouble, but if the sea is smooth, then prosperity and fortune will follow.

Sea serpent—This foretells a deadly enemy who is determined to harm you. To dream that you kill a serpent indicates that you will overcome your enemies and be successful in love and business.

Shark—To dream of a shark predicts an enemy or rival in your life; if the shark eats or swallows you, then the enemy will ruin you.

Shaving—To dream that a person is shaving you indicates a treacherous lover and great disappointment.

Sheaves—To dream that you see a field full of sheaves of corn is a favorable dream, indicating prosperity and a very happy marriage. If you dream that you are gathering the sheaves, it is a sign that you will acquire wealth through your own hard work.

Sheep—To dream you see sheep grazing is a sign of great prosperity and enjoyment. To dream you see them scattered indicates that you will meet with obstacles and trouble.

Shepherd—If you dream you are a shepherd feeding your flocks, it indicates success in work and business.

Shipwreck—To dream you have been shipwrecked is a sign of trials and setbacks. To a lover, it is a sign of disappointment in love. To dream you see others shipwrecked is a dream of opposites; some of your friends or relatives will be promoted or advance in the world.

Shirt—To dream of your shirt being torn indicates gossip or slander; if you tear it, it shows you will make a thoughtless or inappropriate comment. If you dream that your shirt is whole it predicts success in your work.

Shoes—To dream that you have a new pair of shoes is a sign that you will travel frequently. If you dream that your shoes hurt you, it means you will be unsuccessful in your work or business ventures. To dream you are barefoot indicates that you will enjoy comfort and respect in life.

Shooting—To dream that you shoot a bird is a very good omen, indicating success for everyone in their chosen field. If you dream that you shoot and miss, it is a bad sign. It indicates that you will be unsuccessful in business. To dream that you shoot a bird of prey is a sign that you will conquer your enemies.

Shop—To dream that you run a shop is a sign of moderate comfort. You will achieve success through industry and perseverance. To dream that you are working in a shop with another person is a sign that you will meet a kind and charming partner.

Shower—To dream of being in the shower signifies great success in your current plans.

Sickness—To dream that you are sick signifies health; but to dream that you are recovering from sickness is a sign of poor health. To dream that any of your friends or relatives is sick indicates their good health.

Silk—To dream that you see, buy, or sell silk is an omen of good fortune.

Silver—To dream of small silver coins indicates distress; to dream of large coins indicates that you will do lucrative work. To dream that you are buying or selling with silver is a sign of good business. If you dream that the silver is not real it is a sign indicating a false friend or lover.

Singing—It is a dream of opposites, and foretells tears and sadness. To dream that you hear others singing indicates that a friend or relative will be distressed, and that you will suffer through their sadness.

Skating—To dream you are skating indicates success in your business and affairs; but if you fall, or the ice breaks, it shows loss and misfortune. If someone trips you, then beware of an enemy.

Sky—To dream the sky is clear and bright indicates health, wealth, and prosperity; but if the sky is cloudy, it signifies passing trouble. The darker the clouds, the greater the trouble.

Slander—To dream that you are slandered or gossiped about is a dream to the contrary. It means that you will be highly respected.

Slaughterhouse—To dream of a slaughterhouse is very bad; if you see the dead carcasses of animals, it is a sign of sickness and heavy misfortune.

Snake—To dream of snakes is a sure sign of enemies in your life. If you dream that you are stepping on them, don't worry, your enemies will not be able to hurt you. If they run from you, you will overcome them; but if they turn and bite you, it indicates dangerous enemies who will cause you a great deal of trouble.

Sneeze—This dream is unimportant.

Snow—To dream that you see the ground covered in snow is a sign of prosperity. To dream that you are in a snow storm is a good dream. You will face obstacles but will overcome them and be successful.

Soldiers—To dream that you are a soldier foretells that you will change jobs frequently. To dream that you see soldiers fighting indicates that you will be involved in a serious dispute.

Son—To dream that your son is obedient and thoughtful indicates he will be careless, reckless, and vice versa.

Sparrows—To dream you see sparrows hopping around your doorstep indicates that your current projects will go well.

Spider—To dream you see a spider coming towards you indicates someone will pay you some money; to dream the spider is hanging from a thread near you has a similar meaning—you will amass a large fortune.

Splendor—For a person to dream they live in splendor and luxury indicates they will experience severe trials.

Spring—To dream of spring indicates good fortune, success, and a long life.

Stars—For a traveler to dream they see stars clearly is good news, but if the stars are distant or blurred it is a sign of mischief and deception.

Starving—To dream you are starving indicates success and abundance.

Stealing—To dream that you are accused of stealing indicates you will receive a lovely present. If you dream you are guilty of stealing, it means you will experience trouble and hardship.

Steps—To dream that you are climbing stairs indicates that you will rise in life.

Sting—To dream of being stung by a bee or wasp foretells that you will be hurt by cruel people.

Stockings—To dream that you lose your stockings denotes troubles and distress; if there are holes in them be careful of your behavior and what you say.

Storm—To dream of a storm predicts obstacles and misfortune, but they will be short-lived.

Storytelling—To dream of telling a story to a child signifies that you will be respected in powerful circles. To dream of hearing someone else tell a story indicates the loss of one of your senses, likely hearing.

Struggling—To dream you are struggling with a burglar or another dangerous person indicates that you will be respected.

Stumble—If you dream that you stumble, but do not fall, it foretells success in your undertaking. But if you fall down, it is a dream of misfortune.

Success—To dream you are successful in anything is a bad omen, as it indicates the reverse.

Suffocated—To dream that you are suffocated indicates you will be healthy and well.

Sugar—To dream of eating sugar indicates you will experience need and lack—it is an unfavorable dream for anyone.

Sun—To dream of seeing the sun foretells success in work and in love. To dream that you see it rise indicates good news; to see it set, bad news. To dream that you see the sun eclipsed or overcast is a sign of trouble and changes.

Swan—To dream of a white swan signifies wealth and happiness; a black one, trouble at home and grief.

Sweetheart—It you dream that your absent sweetheart is beautiful and attractive, it is a sign of faithfulness and goodness. If you dream that your sweetheart looks haggard, it is a sign that they are not faithful or are being deceptive.

Swimming—To dream you are swimming with your head above water indicates great success in your goals and ambitions. To dream you are swimming with your head under water signifies obstacles and trouble in business. If you sink, it means ruin.

Talking—To dream that you are talking loudly about someone you dislike indicates you will have many difficulties in life. To dream someone is talking about you indicates the reverse—you will have good luck.

Tar—To dream of tar indicates you will travel by water. If you dream you get it on your hands or clothes, it foreshows difficulties.

Tears—*(See Weeping.)*

Teasing—To dream that you are teasing anyone indicates trouble and sickness. To dream someone is teasing you signifies you will soon hear some good news.

Teeth—To dream that you see a person with good teeth indicates that you will marry a beautiful person. To dream that your teeth are loose is a sign of sickness; to dream that one of them comes out indicates the loss of a friend or relative; to dream that they all fall out is a sign of death.

Tempest—This dream indicates many troubles and losses, but you will overcome them and recover.

Temptation—To dream you fall into temptation indicates you will be honorable and thoughtful, and will be well respected by those who know you.

Terror—*(See Afraid.)*

Thatch—To dream that you live in a thatched house means you will rise above your present position through hard work and dedication to your business.

Theatre—*(See Play.)*

Thieves—To dream of thieves is a bad sign: it indicates loss in all cases.

Thorns—To dream of thorns signifies grief, care, and difficulties.

Threshing—To dream you are threshing corn is a sign of success. But if there is little corn, then your hopes will not be met.

Thunder—To see lightning and hear thunder implies that you will be exposed to risk and danger. If you dream that you see lightning and hear thunder at a distance, it indicates that you will overcome all enemies and dangers, and will become very successful in business.

Tiger—To dream that you are attacked by this wild animal indicates an enemy or rival. If you escape, all will be well, but if not your rival will win.

Timber—To dream of timber predicts business and success.

Tipsy—For a person to dream they are tipsy indicates that a new friend will help them and lead them to success.

Toads—For a businessperson this dream indicates fierce competition at work. To dream that you kill a toad indicates success and triumph.

Tomb—To dream that you are walking among tombs foretells marriage. If you dream that you are ordering your own tomb, it indicates that you will shortly be married. But if you see that a tomb has fallen into disrepair and ruin it indicates the reverse.

Torture—To dream that you are being tortured indicates that you will be blessed with happiness and love in the future.

Tower—To dream you are ascending a very high tower

signifies you will experience a reversal in your life and will become poor. Eventually your fortune will change for the better.

Train—To dream of a train predicts travel or the arrival of a dear friend.

Trap—If you fall into a trap, beware of loss through legal matters. If you see traps laid for you, it indicates anxiety.

Traveling—If you dream that you are traveling through a forest and are blocked by the undergrowth and snagged by the trees it signifies obstacles and setbacks. To travel over high hills, mountains, and rocky places indicates that you will advance, but only after many years of hard work.

Treasure—To dream you find a buried treasure indicates that you will succeed in your undertakings and become rich.

Trees—To dream you see beautiful trees with green foliage, or fruit trees in bloom, or trees full of fruit is a sign of unusual prosperity in business or work. To dream you see trees cut down is a sign of the loss of a friend or relative. To dream of climbing trees implies that your life will be an uphill climb.

Trout—To dream of catching trout is an excellent omen; it indicates money. The larger the trout, the more you will receive.

Trumpet—To dream you are playing the trumpet is a sign of prosperity. But if you dream you hear the sound of a trumpet it indicates coming trouble.

Trunk—To dream about a full trunk indicates that you will benefit from your thriftiness. An empty trunk indicates poverty.

Tub—To dream of a tub is a bad omen. If it is filled with water, you should be cautious of evil signs. An empty tub indicates trouble and misfortune.

Tuberculosis—To dream you have this lingering disease indicates you will be healthy and have a long life.

Tunnels—To be in a tunnel indicates anxiety and misfortune, but it will be short-lived.

Turnips—To dream of being in a turnip field, or that you see these vegetables, indicates riches and an important career. For the lover they predict faithfulness.

Ugly—For a person to dream of being ugly indicates that they will hear from a long-absent friend.

Ulcer—To dream that you have ulcers on any part of your body indicates that you will enjoy good health, and live to a good old age.

Umbrella—To dream you borrowed an umbrella signifies sorrow and pain; if you lose your umbrella, expect a severe loss.

Unfortunate—For one who gambles to dream that they have been unfortunate indicates that if they are careful they will become wealthy.

Valentine—For a young person to dream of having received a valentine from a lover indicates misfortune will visit them. To dream of sending a valentine to anyone indicates you will hear of the death of a dear friend.

Valley—To dream you are walking in a pleasant valley and admiring the beauties of nature indicates you will be sick for a time but will recover well.

Vegetables—To dream you are cooking vegetables indicates you will be confused by the strange behavior of someone you are very interested in. To dream that you are eating vegetables signifies sickness.

Vermin—To dream that you see vermin foretells sickness; but if you dream that you get rid of them, restoration to health.

Victory—To dream that you win over an opponent indicates success in other endeavors.

Violence—To dream you have been treated violently by someone who should care for you indicates that you will advance in social standing and importance.

Violin—To dream that you hear the music of a violin is a sign that you will soon be a guest at a social gathering. If the music is accompanied by dancing it indicates prosperity and couples finding happiness in marriage.

Viper—It indicates that you are surrounded by rivals and competitors who will try to outdo you. It also indicates an unfaithful partner.

Vision—To dream that you see a person in a vision means that you will suddenly lose the person you have seen. To dream you see places, property, or anything valuable in a vision indicates disappointment, poverty, and misery.

Visit—To dream you are visiting a friend indicates that you will receive good news that a dear friend is recovering from a severe illness.

Voice—To dream that you hear happy voices foretells distress and weeping. To dream you hear sad or despairing voices is a sign of coming joy.

Volcano—To dream of a volcano foretells conflict, family fighting, and lovers' quarrels.

Vomiting—To dream you are attacked with nausea and vomiting indicates wealth for the poor and for the rich, loss of wealth and property.

Voyage—*(See Traveling.)*

Vulture—To dream you see a vulture is a bad dream. Someone is seeking to undermine your character and reputation. Your rival is dead set against you so be cautious.

Wading—If you dream of wading in a clear stream you will marry soon, but if the stream is muddy you will make unreliable friends.

Wages—If you dream your salary has decreased, you will soon move to a more lucrative position. But if you dream you are making more money, you will soon find yourself out of work.

Wagon—To dream that you are driving a wagon is a sign of poverty; however, if the vehicle is your own, it predicts that you will advance. To dream of riding in a wagon indicates that your reputation will suffer.

Wail—*(See Weeping.)*

Walking—To dream you are walking in the dirt indicates sickness. To dream you are walking through water indicates grief and trouble. To dream you walk at night signifies loss.

Walls—To dream of a barrier or wall you cannot climb indicates trouble at work and embarrassment in family life. To dream that you are walking on a high, narrow wall foretells a risky endeavor. If the wall falls or you descend without being injured, it means you will find success.

Walnuts—To dream of walnuts is a sign of difficulties and troubles in life.

Want—*(See Poverty.)*

War—This is not a good dream. It indicates competition at work and strife in family life.

Warehouse—To dream of being in a warehouse is a good sign for businesspeople and indicates that they will become successful through their hard work and effort.

Warrant—To dream that a warrant has been issued for your arrest signifies you will never be accused of any crime, but will live at peace and be well respected.

Warrior—*(See Soldier.)*

Washing—To dream that you are washing yourself is a good sign meaning that things will change for the better. If you have been sick, this dream indicates a speedy recovery.

Wasps—*(See Sting.)*

Water—To dream you are drinking clean, clear water is favorable; but if it is dirty, it is a very bad sign.

Waves—To dream you are on the beach surrounded by the waves indicates you will find yourself in upsetting and difficult circumstances that will take all your effort and ability to escape.

Wealth—To dream that you have great wealth indicates that sickness and perhaps death are about to visit you or someone you care for.

Weaving—To dream you are weaving fabric indicates success at work.

Wedding—To dream of a wedding is a sign of a funeral. To dream that you are married is a dream of opposites, denoting a life of singleness. For a sick person to dream of being married foretells their death.

Weeding—To dream that you are picking weeds in a garden signifies health, wealth, and a long life.

Weeping—To dream that you are crying is a sign that you will have reasons to be joyful. Your work will be successful in many ways.

Wheat—To dream that you see a field of ripe wheat is a sign that you will grow very rich, and eventually retire.

Whip—To dream that you whip a horse or animal indicates sorrow and trouble.

Whirlpool—To dream that you are in danger of being drowned in a whirlpool indicates adversity and anxiety.

Whirlwind—To dream you are in danger of being swept up by a whirlwind indicates trouble.

Wife—To dream that you are a wife is a sign that you will be one.

Wind—To dream of a brisk wind indicates good news. If you dream of storm winds it indicates troubles and trials in love.

Windmill—To dream you see a windmill indicates that your fortunes will change for the better.

Window—To dream that you are seated at a window, looking at the passersby, indicates you will be harassed by gossip and lies.

Wine—To dream that you are drinking wine is a sign of health, wealth, long life, and happiness. To dream that you are drinking wine with other people indicates a coming celebration. If you are in business it will prove very lucrative.

Wings—To dream that you have wings indicates deep sadness.

Witchcraft—For a person to dream they have visited a fortune teller indicates they will experience misfortune; fighting at home, backstabbing at work, and deception from close friends.

Wolf—To dream of being chased by a wolf indicates you will be troubled by a lying enemy; if it catches you it will be worse.

Wood—*(See Timber.)*

Wool—To dream you are buying or selling wool indicates prosperity and wealth. To the lover, it is a good sign.

Work—To dream you are working hard and are exhausted indicates sickness. If you see others at work, it indicates successful business. If you dream you are working with your right hand, it signifies good fortune. Working with the left hand predicts momentary embarrassment.

Worms—To dream that you see a large number of worms in your path indicates the death of yourself or a very dear friend.

Wounds—To dream you are wounded is a very favorable omen, especially if by a sword.

Wreath—To dream that you have a wreath on your head indicates that you will overcome difficulties and find success.

Wreck—*(See Shipwreck.)*

Writing—To dream you are writing a letter, whether for love or business, indicates you will be surprised to receive a letter from a friend you haven't heard from in many years.

Yarn—To dream you are spinning yarn is good; it means you will receive a lovely present from a dear friend.

Yawning—To dream you are continually yawning indicates you will make slow progress in life and never become rich.

Yew tree—This dream indicates the death of someone from whom you will receive a large inheritance. If you dream that you sit under a yew tree, it foretells that your life will be short. But if you merely look at and admire it, you will have a long life.

Young—To dream of young people is a sign of domestic happiness. To dream that you are young is a sign of sickness.

Zodiac—To dream of the twelve signs of the zodiac indicates that you will be a great traveler and go around the world at least once.

PART II
INTERPRETING CIPHERS

METHOD OF WORKING THE DREAMS

The second form of dream interpretation relies on ciphers, which are really just rows of marks (dashes, circles, crosses, or whatever mark you prefer) arranged in a particular pattern. To interpret your dream, you will create four different ciphers. The first cipher, the Intuitive cipher, will be used to create the following three—the First Sign, the Second Sign, and the Index—which will guide you to the specific meaning of your dream. Let's begin!

The first step is to jot down ten rows of marks—just a row of dots or lines—as shown below. Don't count them as you go or try to make any sort of pattern. Simply make ten rows without any thought or agenda, following your intuition as you go. The marks will feel random, but they are anything but. This is your Intuitive cipher.

Next, you will create a new cipher, called the First Sign, derived from the Intuitive cipher. Count the number of marks in the Intuitive cipher to determine whether there is an even or odd number of marks in each row. If the number of marks in a row is odd, add a single mark in the corresponding line of your new cipher, but if it's even, add two marks. So if your Intuitive cipher was composed of lines that were:

Row One: Odd
Row Two: Even
Row Three: Odd

Your First Sign cipher would have one mark on Row One, two marks on Row Two, and one mark on Row Three. Repeat this process, marking the first five lines of your Intuitive cipher even or odd to create the First Sign cipher.

Then go through lines 6–10 of your Intuitive cipher in the same way, counting the marks in each line, and marking them down as odd or even. This will give the Second Sign.

Here's an example of the whole process:

INTUITIVE CIPHER			SIGN 1
1. OOOOOOOOOOOOOO,	in all 14 ciphers,	even,	O O
2. OOOOOOOOO,	in all 10 ciphers,	even,	O O
3. OOOOOOOOOOOOO,	in all 13 ciphers,	odd,	O
4. OOOOOOOOOOO,	in all 11 ciphers,	odd,	O
5. OOOOOOO,	in all 7 ciphers,	odd,	O

Those five lines of ciphers make the First Sign.

INTUITIVE CIPHER			SIGN 2
6. OOOOOO,	in all 6 ciphers,	even,	O O
7. OOOOOOOO,	in all 8 ciphers,	even,	O O
8. OOOOOOOOOOO,	in all 11 ciphers,	odd,	O
9. OOOOOOOOOOO,	in all 11 ciphers,	odd,	O
10. OOOOOOOOOOOOO,	in all 13 ciphers,	odd,	O

Lines 6–10 make up the Second Sign.

Now that you've created the First and Second sign, you will create a fourth and final cipher, called the Index. Begin by rewriting the First and Second ciphers and placing them side by side (as shown below). Once again, count the number of marks in each line (combining the marks in the First and Second ciphers) and designate them as odd or even with one mark or two marks depending. This is your new cipher, the Index.

SIGN 1		SIGN 2		INDEX
O O	..	O O	..	even O O
O O	..	O O	..	even O O
O	..	O	..	even O O
O	..	O	..	even O O
O	..	O	..	even O O

And now the counting is done! Compare your Index cipher to the list of ciphers below and find the category that corresponds with your cipher. For instance, the category for the Index above is Aries. Once you know the category, whether it's Cancer or Jove or Ceres etc.—simply flip to that section of the book and find the dream interpretation that corresponds with your First and Second ciphers. Refer to the example below, but with a little practice you'll be able to create all four ciphers quickly and easily!

TABLE OF INDEXES

The following are the tabular names of the Indexes which are at the head of each page:

ARIES	SOLEIL	TAURUS	JOVE	GEMINI	LUNA
CANCER	SATURN	LEO	MARS	VIRGO	MERCURY
LIBRA	VENUS	SCORPIO	PALLAS	SAGITTARIUS	JUNO

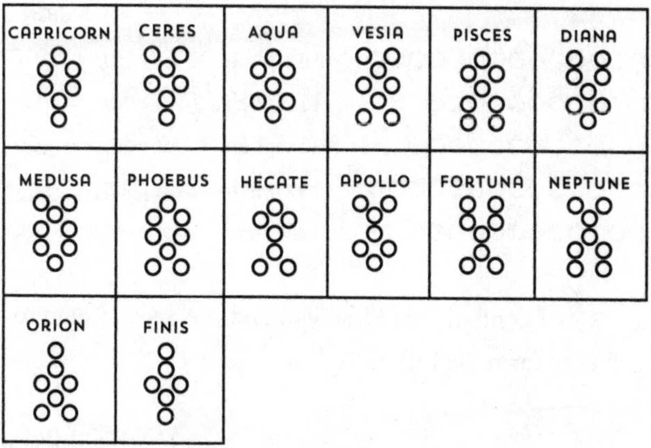

CAPRICORN	CERES	AQUA	VESIA	PISCES	DIANA
MEDUSA	PHOEBUS	HECATE	APOLLO	FORTUNA	NEPTUNE
ORION	FINIS				

AN EXAMPLE READING

If I wish to know the meaning of a particularly vivid dream, I begin by making ten rows of marks to create the Intuitive cipher:

			SIGN 1
OOOOOOOOOOOO,	12 ciphers,	or even,	O O
OOOOOOOOO,	9 ciphers,	or odd,	O
OOOOOOOOOOOOOOO,	15 ciphers ,	or odd,	O
OOOOOO,	6 ciphers,	or even,	O
OOOOOOOOOO,	10 ciphers,	or even,	O O

			SIGN 2
OOOOOOOOOOOOOO,	14 ciphers,	or even,	O O
OOOOOOOOOOO,	11 ciphers,	or odd,	O
OOOOOOOOOOOOO,	13 ciphers ,	or odd,	O
OOOOOOOOOOOOOO,	14 ciphers,	or even,	O O
OOOOOOOOOOOO	12 ciphers,	or even,	O O

Now I combine the First Sign and the Second Sign together to form the Index.

					INDEX
O O	O O	=	4 ciphers,	or even	O O
O	O	=	2 ciphers,	or even	O O
O	O	=	2 ciphers,	or even	O O
O O	O O	=	4 ciphers,	or even	O O
O O	O O	=	4 ciphers,	or even	O O

With this Index, I refer to the Table of Indexes, and find this Sign: O O / O O / O O / O O refers to the Hieroglyphic Emblem of Aries.

Then I turn to the Interpretations and find Aries, which is on page 123, and from the Signs I look for the patterns of the First and Second Signs I created: and find the corresponding dream interpretation. In this case I learn that

O O	O O
O	O
O	O
O O	O O
O O	O O

my dream refers to: An uncommon omen; trouble and hard work are coming. Expect a difficult time and be very careful.

HIEROGLYPHIC EMBLEM

ARIES

SIGN 1. 2.	
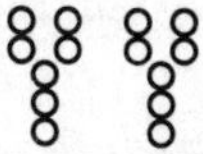	Your dream signifies that your fate is about to undergo a change for the better: fortune and friends await you.
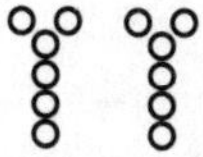	This is a happy and joyful dream; it predicts celebration, festivities, and happiness.
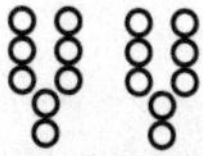	An unfavorable dream; prepare for disappointments in your business or in your love life.
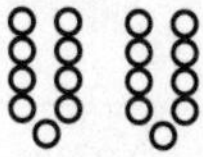	Beware of enemies; avoid tall, thin men, with watchful eyes and a dejected look.
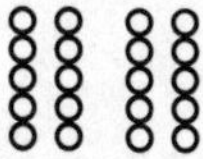	Prepare for change. This signifies traveling, voyages, and moving from place to place.
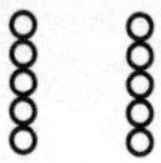	An insignificant dream—portending little or nothing important.

SIGN 1.	SIGN 2.	*ARIES*
		Beware of anger and contention, avoid quarrels and the law. Be careful.
		This is a dream of business, prosperity, abundance, and impressive accomplishments.
		This is a dream of traveling, but avoid leaving home. You risk accidents and danger.
		A cheerful dream denoting joy, pleasure, and conviviality.
		Expect to hear news of distant friends or relatives.
		A dream of funerals, the burying of the dead; of sorrow and grief.
		You have a secret enemy who is attempting to undermine you. Beware!
		Beware of coming alarm or anxiety; avoid danger, and stay home for a time.
		This dream foretells marriage, joy, and the company of women.

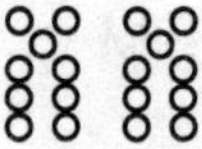

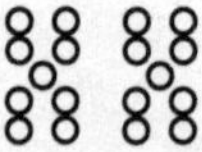

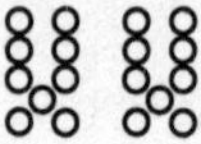

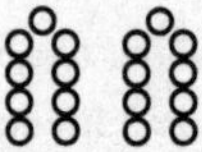

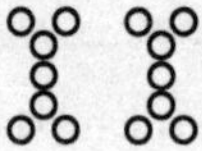

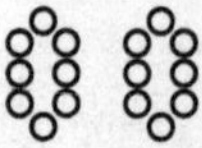

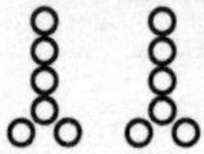

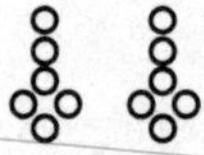

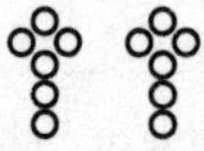

SIGN 1. 2.	*ARIES*
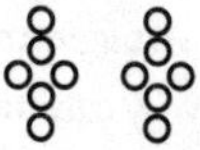	Predicts joy, love, companionship, and accomplishing your aspirations.
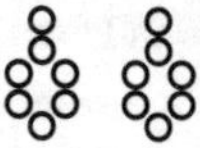	Your dream is very sad and ominous. Beware of bereavement, of grief, and of tears.
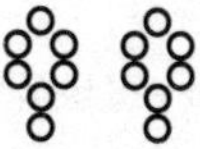	Misfortune is at hand. Prepare yourself. Avoid speculation, and don't attempt anything risky.
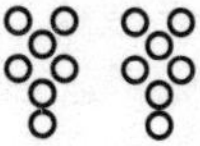	This dream forebodes happiness and good fortune; you will meet your goals and fulfill your hopes.
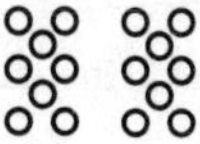	Good fortune awaits the dreamer. Expect growth and profit in your business beyond your most ambitious expectations.
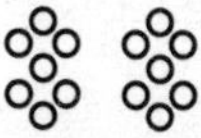	To those in love this dream foretells frustration and difficulty; for someone in business it predicts disappointment.
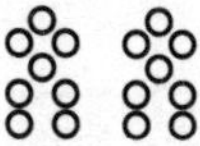	Expect significant and unpredictable setbacks. Your purposes are thwarted, and will not be accomplished.
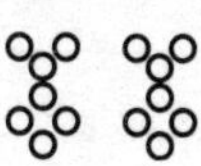	Expect a journey after this dream, and an unsettled time for some months.

SIGN 1.	2.	*ARIES*
		An uncommon omen; hard work and struggle are coming. Expect a difficult time and be very careful.
		Beware of losses! Guard against thieves and fire. A bad dream for possessions and money; it threatens sudden loss.
		Disappointment is on the horizon; you will be deceived.
		A good dream! You will prosper, and your business will increase.
		A sorrowful dream! A funeral is probable in your family, or the loss of a sincere friend.
		The loss of a valued friend is predicted; this is a dream of grief and sorrow.
		This dream foretells the friendship of powerful people.
		Fortune is fickle. Your dream predicts sudden changes in your welfare, gains, losses, and confusion.
		A victorious dream! You will overcome an adversary whom you fear.

HIEROGLYPHIC EMBLEM

SOL

SIGN 1.	SIGN 2.	
		Prepare for a trip in the near future; travel is indicated.
		This dream foretells a heaviness of spirit, despondency, and lack of hope in the future.
		Your dream foretells unease; work and worry will be a burden for a time.
		Beware! A faithless friend is near you, and will cause you trouble.
		This is a dream of fighting, legal issues, contention, and perhaps bloodshed. Beware of arguments, and take care not to offend.
		Confusion and evasiveness are signified by this dream.

SIGN 1.	2.	*SOL*
		Beware of bodily illness; stay calm and don't become overly anxious or nervous.
		On the first day of the moon this dream foretells an inheritance; at other times, friends.
		Beware of treachery and deceit. At the same time you can expect a gift.
		On a Saturday this dream indicates trouble and sorrow; on other days it is unimportant.
		Beware of speculation! Don't risk your money after this dream and avoid making any bets.
		This dream signifies that the worst is past, your troubles are nearly over, and that better fortune is in store for you.
		Heavy, frustrating, and difficult times may be expected; the star of your destiny is clouded.
		Expect sad news; the sickness or loss of a relative or a very kind friend.
		Prepare for a wedding! Joy and laughter are at hand.

SIGN 1.	SIGN 2.	*SOL*
		The love of a fair woman is at hand; or a marriage.
		You have a thief living near you; take care that he does not rob you.
		The end of joy is sadness, as you will find. Your dream is not beneficial. Be careful.
		This suggests the imprisonment of a friend, which will cause you great sadness.
		Don't move house after this dream, or you will regret your move.
		Anger, quarreling, and conflict are signified by this dream. You will be disappointed in your hopes.
		An absent friend is about to visit you; prepare to receive them.
		Gossipers are talking—and they're talking about you! Beware of rumors.
		The star of your destiny is clouded, and for a time misfortune and trouble will haunt you.

SIGN 1.	SIGN 2.	*SOL*
		On the third and sixth days of the month this dream is favorable, but at other times it indicates evil and disappointment.
		Expect a trip in a very short time; it will relate to important matters connected with your welfare.
		A dream of wealth! You will have great material abundance, for the star of your destiny shines bright.
		A friend is announced. You are born to fortune. Be happy, for your dream is auspicious.
		To the sailor it foretells a rough voyage; to others, a stormy time in their affairs.
		You will find treasure; or you will discover something that has been lost.
		You will receive an inheritance within three years. Your dream is a good omen.
		For three years you will be prosperous. Look! The star of your fortune has risen.

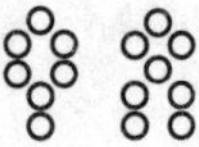

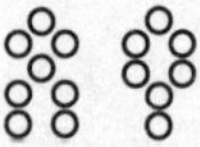

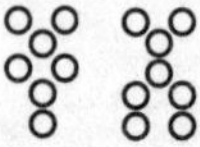

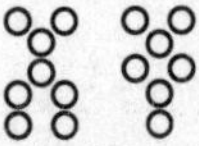

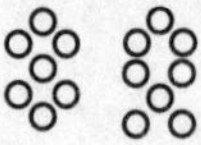

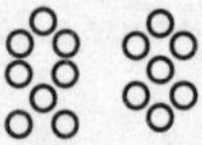

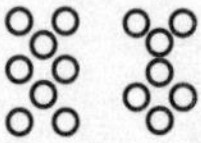

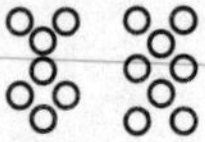

HIEROGLYPHIC EMBLEM

TAURUS

SIGN 1.	SIGN 2.	
		A dream of obscurity, presented by an unsettled mind. It's not significant.
		Trouble is at hand; it will be severe, but will pass quickly.
		To dream this on a Saturday forebodes misfortune, but on other days this is a good sign.
		A dream of money, which the dreamer will shortly receive.
		Major expenses are predicted; losing or paying large amounts of money.
		Trouble in money matters is approaching; danger of a loss, and frustration in your business.

SIGN 1.	SIGN 2.	*TAURUS*
		New friends await you and will make you welcome; their friendship will benefit you.
		Observe your actions; you have an enemy watching you who means you harm.
		Beware of deceit, guile, sadness, the ill will of private enemies, and treachery.
		Beware! Your dream forebodes sorrow; your hopes and expectations will be thwarted.
		Letters and paperwork will annoy you and will bring you bad news.
		Rivals in business and rivals in love are signified by this dream, but they will not overcome you.
		An unlucky omen. The star of your fortune is clouded, and misfortune awaits you; don't irritate your enemies.
		A tall, lean, saturnine person is seeking to do you injury; take caution and avoid them.
		You have dreamed well! Joy and good news are on their way; your wishes shall be gratified.

SIGN 1.	SIGN 2.	*TAURUS*
		Prepare for travel; before long you will take a trip that will bring you good fortune.
		Trips are in your future; the arrival of long absent friends; agitation and stirring things up.
		A grievous dream—misfortune is at hand. You will have to carry a heavy burden.
		This dream indicates loss through neglect or a lack of caution in your work; be careful.
		Be careful in how you word what you say and write, because this dream predicts trouble from that quarter.
		An unfortunate dream for all things. If in love, expect disappointment and sorrow; if in business, misfortune.
		A favorable vision—you can expect success in love and in your business.
		A train of planetary influence is approaching that will give you mixed fortune. If you are a lover this is a sign of trouble.

SIGN 1.	SIGN 2.	*TAURUS*
		You will receive a message with bad news that will upset you.
		Your reputation is on trial; false rumors will be circulated. Be alert!
		Be careful of deceitful friends; those whom you trust most will prove your greatest enemies.
		Sickness is about to enter your home.
		You will be annoyed by some paperwork or documents—they will not arrive in time.
		Letters and hasty news are approaching. You will hear news from someone who has long been silent.
		A fortunate dream. Your fate is about to change for the better, and prosperity awaits you.
		Prepare yourself for loss and disappointment. If in love, you will be ill-fated, and lose the object of your affections.
		A pleasant dream, denoting celebration, joy, and prosperity—the object of your affections is sincere.

HIEROGLYPHIC EMBLEM

JOVE

SIGN 1.	SIGN 2.	
		Your dream signifies change is at hand.
		The dreamer may expect to go on a trip, and may cross a body of water—so prepare.
		Expect a loss if you dreamed this on the third day of the month, as it is unfortunate.
		Your dream is full of misfortune. Be careful with your home.
		Be careful what you write, as your messages are being intercepted.
		The omens are poor; expect sorrow or family troubles.

SIGN 1.	SIGN 2.	*JOVE*
		These are signs that the place you are visiting will hold trouble.
		Unless you were careless in divining the omens, you can expect to experience fear or anxiety.
		Your dream signifies a future loss in your life.
		This dream indicates scandals, and frustration at the cares of life.
		A grievance that you thought was forgotten will return with renewed vigor.
		You may expect anger, or angry words from this vision.
		Dreamer, rejoice! Trouble no longer threatens to overwhelm you; your fortune is more favorable.
		Your dream signifies extraordinary news from friends, and predicts that you will be busy for the next three months.
		This vision is ill-omened and bad.

SIGN 1.	SIGN 2.	*JOVE*
		There will be peril, grief, or a secret illness in your home. Beware!
		Be careful! The signs suggest riding on horseback, or spending time with animals, but it will not end well.
		Expect old grievances to be suddenly renewed. Your dream is not good.
		Your dream portends a marriage or celebration.
		This dream involves joy and laughter.
		This dream suggests that you will shortly receive a delightful invitation.
		Your dream is one of sorrow and misfortunes.
		You will be subject to evil influences, which you would do well to guard against.
		You can expect a new and beneficial friendship in your life in the next month.

SIGN 1.	SIGN 2.	*JOVE*
		After this dream you may expect a loss; especially if you dreamed on the third day of the month.
		Be careful! Avoid the arguments that this dream foretells.
		You'll meet three people this year who will become dear and loyal friends.
		This dream has various meanings; if you are single, it indicates marriage.
		If your dream was alarming, don't worry—it doesn't foretell anything negative.
		Be careful what you say to others; this dream predicts angry words.
		The coming days will not be your most successful.
		Regardless of the nature of your dream, nothing bad will happen.

HIEROGLYPHIC EMBLEM

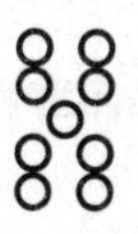

GEMINI

SIGN 1.	SIGN 2.	
		Your dream foreshows a journey, or crossing deep waters.
		This foretells an increase in business, and having to deal with books, paperwork, and writing.
		Your dream predicts that a cause of annoyance and irritation will be gone before long.
		This dream indicates that something you have long wished for has passed you by.
		Your dream signifies good fortune, winning, and a full bank account.
		This dream predicts that you will soon make a profitable bargain.

SIGN 1.	SIGN 2.	*GEMINI*
		This dream will give you victory over enemies or obstacles.
		This dream foretells that you will shortly be invited to a joyful event.
		Beware! There are liars among your friends, and you will encounter sickness where you travel.
		Your enemies may be liars and cheaters, but your dream foretells that you will be victorious.
		You have dreamed a bad dream. Whatever you planned for tomorrow, brace for trouble.
		This dream predicts messages, letters, and long absent friends.
		Your dream is one of sadness and sorrow.
		Death threatens to rob you of a near and dear companion.
		Your dream is playful and joyful; it may also carry good fortune.

SIGN 1.	SIGN 2.	*GEMINI*
		This dream speaks of regret over things that have passed away.
		Lock your door; this dream predicts theft.
		Beware! Rivals who mean you harm are nearby.
		Your dream signifies marriage to someone tall and fair within the year.
		Unless you dreamt on the first day of the month, or during a lunar eclipse, you can expect significant gain.
		This dream foretells the love of a beautiful woman.
		Your dream suggests trouble is coming. Be on your guard.
		Your dream verges upon evil.
		You must be careful, as this dream predicts mental unrest and unease.

SIGN 1.	2.	*GEMINI*
		Your dream is evil: something you have expected will not come about.
		Trouble is around the corner and in your home.
		The light of many stars has combined to turn your fortune to good.
		If you dreamt this on a Friday it foretells lies and deceit; on a Monday, a trip; on other days, a new friend.
		The signs are troublesome and difficult.
		This dream comes from sickness.
		Your dream indicates happiness, laughter, and pleasure.
		Your dream is unfavorable. You risk the loss of something you value.

HIEROGLYPHIC EMBLEM

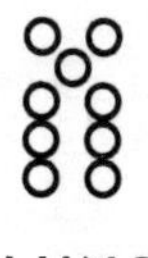

LUNA

SIGN 1.	SIGN 2.	
		Be warned! The stars indicate that someone in your circle is being deceptive.
		Dreamer! Your fears are unfounded; do not worry.
		Your dream promises future wealth.
		This dream foretells seven years of good fortune.
		Buckle up! This dream predicts a coming trip.
		This dream foretells a trip or adventure with a pleasant fellow traveler.

SIGN 1.	SIGN 2.	*LUNA*
		Your dream signifies that some of your absent friends are in trouble.
		You can expect loss in your family.
		Your dream suggests that for a time you'll be occupied with paperwork and books.
		You will soon hear some news from an unreliable source.
		After this dream you should prepare for loss.
		Good times await you. After this dream you can expect to receive some money.
		Prepare for grief.
		Pay attention to your health; you can expect to be sick.
		You have dreamed well; you'll stumble upon a happy windfall.

SIGN 1.	SIGN 2.	*LUNA*
		You will discover a secret.
		You should prepare for sickness and calamity.
		Your dream is bad. Brace yourself for trouble in the future.
		The dream foreshows a move in your future.
		Your dream speaks of confusion relating to contracts and legal documents. Be on your guard or it could lead to a great loss.
		Expect a month of unpleasantness, and beware of monetary loss.
		Be careful in your behavior, as this dream indicates mischief.
		Your dream predicts a funeral within a year.
		Be careful! Good fortune is fickle and may leave you.

SIGN 1.	SIGN 2.	*LUNA*
		Your dream is one of good fortune; it foretells money, gifts, and prosperity.
		You have the golden touch—don't take it for granted.
		Your dream applies to more lives than just your own and it speaks of misfortune.
		Be mindful of your actions; this dream suggests you should take care.
		Your dream was a nightmare, but it predicts only good things.
		Get ready because you will soon find yourself traveling.
		Brace yourself to hear about the illness of a dear friend.
		This dream predicts grief of some kind in your future.

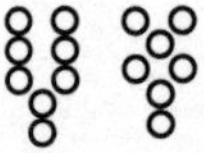

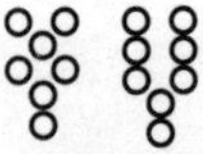

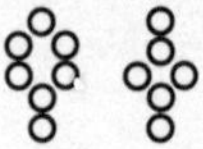

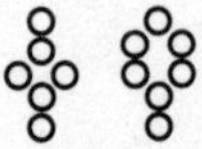

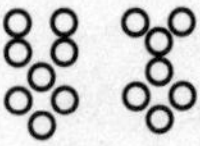

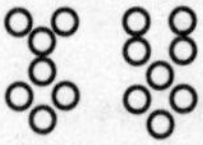

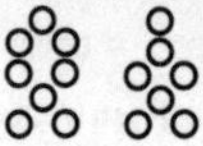

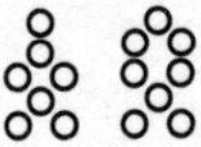

HIEROGLYPHIC EMBLEM

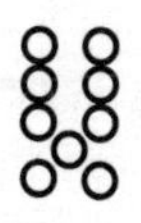

CANCER

Sign 1.	Sign 2.	
		If your dream was about money, it predicts deceit and lies. If not, then it does not mean anything significant.
		Your dream signifies that you will travel on a ship or hear a tale from someone who has.
		Your dream speaks of sadness and difficulty.
		You may soon experience the loss of a friend.
		Prepare for sickness, as you'll be under the weather in a few days.
		This dream foretells sickness and trouble.

SIGN 1.	SIGN 2.	*CANCER*
		Your dream predicts adversaries in your life, but you will overcome them.
		Your dream is one of confusion.
		This dream predicts many strong friendships.
		Your dream signifies joy and celebration. Enjoy yourself!
		Your dream is a bad omen. Be careful and vigilant.
		Be on your guard. Suddenly you will encounter adversity, but you will overcome it.
		Your dream predicts obstacles and setbacks; be on your guard.
		On the first day of the month you can expect a message; on the fourth or sixth, joy; on the thirteenth, a funeral; any other day, sadness.
		Expect to hear good news after this dream.

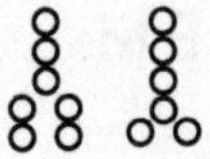

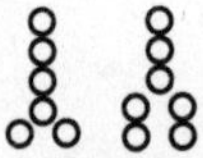

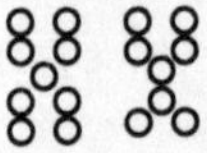

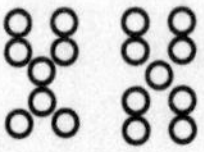

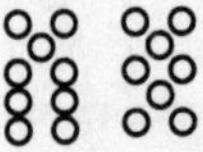

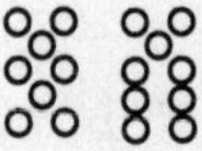

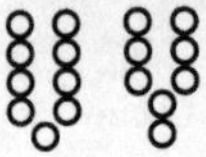

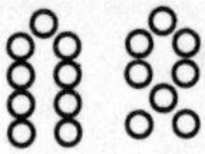

SIGN 1.	2.	*CANCER*
		Look around you, and beware of secrets and liars.
		Your dream foretells disappointment; you will not take a trip you had planned.
		Expect to encounter sadness.
		Your dream foreshows traveling and a journey.
		Your dream foretells first a trip by land and then a journey by boat.
		Your dream may have been a pleasant one, but it predicts betrayal.
		One of your female friends is being duplicitous and you will soon discover how.
		You have dreamed well; your dream is amazingly fortunate.
		Expect money or messages to arrive in your life. This is a favorable dream.

SIGN 1.	SIGN 2.	*CANCER*
		Your dream predicts frustrations and difficulties among friends.
		After this dream you can expect to spend some time sick in bed.
		Something you've undertaken will not work out.
		Your dream is good. Some powerful friends are eager to welcome you.
		Before long you will be very prosperous.
		Your dream is a disappointing one; many things you've hoped for will not happen.
		This is an omen of coming loss.
		This dream is an indicator of coming struggle.

HIEROGLYPHIC EMBLEM

SATURN

SIGN 1.	SIGN 2.	
		This dream is a sign that you will have to attend a funeral.
		You will soon learn that you have lost a friend.
		This dream is a sign that you will achieve something unexpected.
		This is a sign of a coming funeral.
		Your dream foretells a party.
		This dream indicates friendship.

SIGN 1.	SIGN 2.	*SATURN*
		Your dream signifies anger. Be on your guard.
		Something that you expect will not happen.
		Your dream is one of joyfulness and profit in connection with a legal or business matter.
		You can expect to receive an inheritance.
		Beware! Someone you welcomed into your life will prove to be a liar.
		These omens suggest that someone or something in your life is concealing their true nature.
		Your dream is a good sign; you'll quickly find good fortune.
		Your mind and thoughts are anxious and fraught, but your dream predicts good things nonetheless.
		Something you've dreamed of will be accomplished without requiring much effort.

SIGN 1. 2.	*SATURN*
	Your dream warns you to beware of signing contracts, deeds, or other binding documents.
	You will soon receive good things.
	Your dream is a sign of new friends and acquaintances coming into your life.
	Beautiful and kind men will woo you.
	Your dream suggests that you will receive a love letter.
	Even in the midst of difficulties, you are still safe.
	Your dream signifies that you will soon be traveling quickly to an unknown destination.
	Expect change and travel in your future.
	Your dream is unlucky; there are several interpretations but all run counter to your desires.

SIGN 1.	SIGN 2.	*SATURN*
		Your dream foretells great wealth.
		Your dream is very good; good fortune is coming your way—keep going!
		Your dream is a bad omen; expect loss and trouble in your work.
		Double-check the lock on your door; this dream predicts there are thieves nearby.
		You will soon receive a message or unexpected news.
		Your dream foretells money, except on Sunday.
		Be careful with your words; this dream warns of anger.
		Your dream suggests you have a redheaded enemy. Be careful of them.

HIEROGLYPHIC EMBLEM

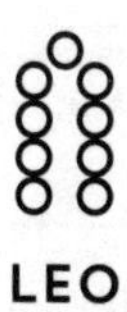

LEO

SIGN 1.	SIGN 2.	
		Your dream suggests you can look forward to good fortune.
		You will make a profitable business deal or receive money from someone overseas.
		You can soon expect a letter, message, or present.
		You will soon meet an honest and loyal friend.
		If you're a businessperson this dream is a sign of money; for everyone else it promises good friendship.
		Wedding bells are ringing! You will marry within the year.

SIGN 1.	SIGN 2.	*LEO*
		Something you've been pursuing will fail, which will deeply disappointment you.
		Your dream predicts trouble; avoid traveling.
		Be careful of lawsuits and other legal matters, as your dream suggests poor outcomes and confusion in that area.
		If you had this dream on the third day of the month, expect the loss of a relative.
		You must be careful, as your dream signifies secret enemies.
		Your dream signifies secret enemies, but you will avoid their interference.
		The signs suggest that a problem from your past that you have long forgotten will return.
		Your dream warns of a loss.
		This is a sign that you will lose a friend or family member in some way.

SIGN 1.	SIGN 2.	*LEO*
		You will soon attend a funeral.
		Be careful what you sign.
		Be mindful of your possessions as thieves are possible.
		Your dream predicts squabbling, but avoid it.
		This signifies anger over a work matter.
		Your dream foretells many changes and a restless feeling.
		You will soon hear some bad news, which will cause you sadness.
		Beware of lies and deception among your friends. Don't put your trust in thoughtless people.
		Your dream is one of anger, strife, and bad news.

SIGN 1.	SIGN 2.	*LEO*
		You can expect good fortune to arrive quickly.
		This dream foretells good news from a friend.
		Your dream predicts loss and sorrow.
		Be on your guard; a secret enemy may be trying to do you harm.
		Even though your dream was a nightmare, it foretells good fortune.
		Prepare for change, as you will take a trip and very likely cross the ocean.
		You will soon hear news from a female friend, and news from a friend in trouble.
		The dreamer will soon take a journey.

HIEROGLYPHIC EMBLEM

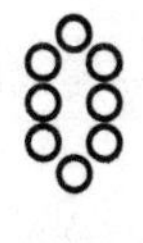

MARS

SIGN 1.	SIGN 2.	
		Your dream suggests grief and tears.
		A distant relation will soon die.
		If you dreamed on a Monday or a Wednesday you will have good fortune.
		Your dream predicts travel—you will go on a long journey.
		This dream foreshows an ample supply of money so you have dreamed well.
		Your dream foretells presents or gifts.

SIGN 1.	SIGN 2.	*MARS*
		Within three weeks of this dream you will meet a new friend.
		Your dream is one of happiness and joy.
		Your dream signifies business, study, and the work of the mind.
		A dark-haired woman will bring you trouble.
		There is nothing more deceitful than this dream. Don't trust a redheaded man.
		You will soon hear from a friend who is ill.
		You may have been going through a hard time, but you will persevere.
		Your dream signifies grief and sorrow.
		Your dream foretells a mix of joy and of sadness.

SIGN 1.	SIGN 2.	*MARS*
		You will experience sadness, but joy will follow.
		Get out your dancing shoes! You'll soon be married or attend a wedding.
		Your dream foreshows a trip if dreamt on the seventh day of the month; on any other day, it promises good friends.
		A sign of conflict relating to a message or other written document.
		Your dream foretells the sudden loss of a dear friend.
		You have had a vision of trouble to come.
		Your dream suggests that trouble will surround you on every side. Be extra careful.
		This dream foretells that you will have disappointments—all relating to money.
		This is a sign that something you are expecting will be delayed.

SIGN 1.	SIGN 2.	*MARS*
		Your dream will bring you good fortune in a short space of time.
		This dream either indicates marriage or deceit among friends.
		Your dream is very good; you will have many months of good fortune.
		You can expect a fight about money.
		You may receive some money in the near future.
		You will soon hear some unexpected news.
		Your dream doesn't imply anything of importance.
		Let the dreamer prepare for some sort of loss, unless it was dreamt on a full moon.

HIEROGLYPHIC EMBLEM

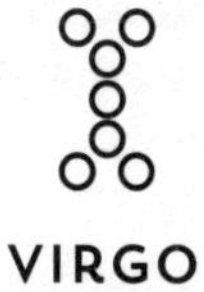

VIRGO

SIGN 1.	SIGN 2.	
		Prepare for travel and busyness, especially if the moon isn't full.
		This dream foretells travel and journeys.
		Your dream suggests an obstacle at work. It will be frustrating.
		You will experience frustration in some part of your life.
		Your dream foretells happiness, marriage, and contentment, especially if dreamed on a Thursday.
		If you dreamed this on the ninth day of the month, be prepared for a thief in your life. On any other day, a friend may be lying to you.

SIGN 1.	SIGN 2.	*VIRGO*
		From your dream I judge that you will be introduced to very rich and influential friends.
		Your dream is good; it will bring about all your hopes and wishes.
		Your dream indicates wealth after poverty; all your wishes will be fulfilled.
		After this dream, you can expect to receive a position of power or prestige.
		Your dream, if it takes place on a Friday, will be very unlucky. Be careful!
		You can expect presents and favors from rich people.
		Your dream foreshows travel, or flitting from one place to another.
		Your dream suggests that you will buy a house or make another significant purchase.
		This dream signifies that your marriage, or a friend's, will be delayed.

SIGN 1.	SIGN 2.	*VIRGO*
		This is a dream of marriage, or anything that pleases the heart.
		Your dream foreshows an unexpected mix of joy, sorrow, hatred, and happiness.
		You have many secret enemies. Be careful of a saturnine person in your life.
		This is a good dream for a sick person, and if the moon is waxing, it foretells that money will come your way.
		Your dream signifies that you will receive a reward for something you've done.
		This dream predicts loss for the wealthy and gain for the poor.
		Your dream means that you will have trouble in love.
		To the sick, this dream predicts continued illness; but to one grieving or struggling, it predicts relief.
		Your dream signifies sickness from overeating.

SIGN 1.	SIGN 2.	*VIRGO*
		Your dream predicts a party, a new outfit, and a celebration.
		You have dreamed well and things will be pleasant and prosperous.
		You will be a fortunate and happy person, unless you dreamt this on the first day of the month.
		Your dream signifies that you will have a long life, without much struggle or adversity.
		Be on your guard against deceitful friends, because they will try to ruin you.
		Your dream indicates fighting and angry words.
		Your dream is very bad; be careful what you say and do.
		Prepare for illness.

HIEROGLYPHIC EMBLEM

MERCURY

SIGN 1.	SIGN 2.	
		If this dream was dreamed on a Friday night, it foretells marriage for a young dreamer and success for an older dreamer.
		Your dream foretells that you will shortly go on a long trip, which will lead to good things.
		Your dream predicts trials and sadness. Troubles will surround you.
		You must beware, as you have an enemy who is trying to do you harm.
		Your dream signifies that you will have riches and wealth in your old age.
		Your dream indicates prosperity and wealth in a few years.

SIGN 1.	SIGN 2.	*MERCURY*
		You will gain wealth, but be careful lest you lose it again.
		You can expect to receive a present of gold or silver.
		During the second half of your life you can expect wealth.
		For a season, you will be very poor due to your own decisions.
		This dream relates to state affairs, and is a sign of trouble in high places.
		This dream signifies that your character may be discredited or maligned.
		Your dream indicates trouble and sadness after a festive occasion.
		You will soon meet a person who will be a sincere friend to you, someone you can truly trust.
		Beware! Your dream suggests theft if you aren't careful to prevent it.

SIGN 1.	SIGN 2.	*MERCURY*
		Your dream foreshows going on a trip or riding on horseback.
		This dream shows departures of a frustrating kind.
		This dream foretells much evil on a Saturday.
		Be careful! You have an evil-minded adversary, but if you are clever you will prevail.
		Your dream predicts success and good health.
		You have a number of personal enemies, so be careful.
		On a Friday, or on the thirteenth day of the month, your dream is unlucky.
		Your dream signifies festivities and a good time.
		This dream anticipates great and abundant wealth for the dreamer.

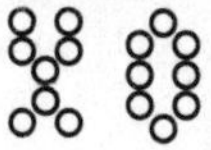

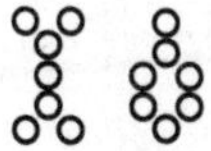

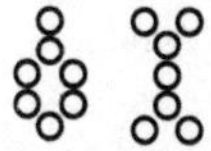

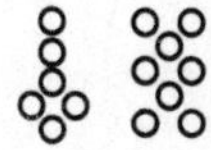

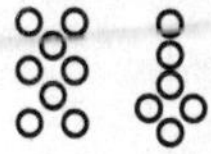

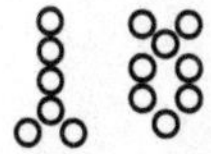

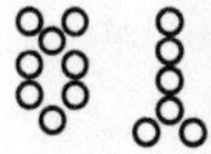

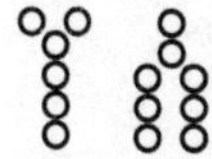

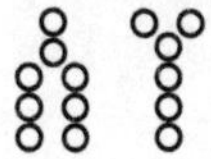

SIGN 1.	SIGN 2.	*MERCURY*
		Your dream is good: it foretells success and honor.
		The dreamer must be careful of horned cattle and all four-footed animals.
		You will soon hear news from absent friends.
		Your dream foretells sickness.
		You will soon do a great deal of walking or go on a trip.
		Your dream relates to business and you will soon receive an inside tip.
		Your dream is bad; for a season you will struggle with money.
		This dream warns against moving house.

HIEROGLYPHIC EMBLEM

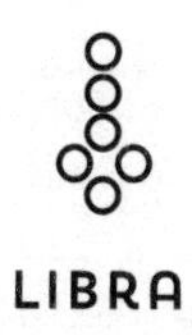

LIBRA

SIGN 1.	SIGN 2.	
		Beware of pickpockets!
		Your dream foretells that you are about to receive an unexpected windfall from someone.
		Get ready for company, as someone who has been traveling will soon appear at your door.
		Good fortune is in store for you. Money will soon come to you in the mail.
		Your dream predicts good fortune for many months.
		Your dream means that business will be good and sales will grow.

SIGN 1.	SIGN 2.	*LIBRA*
		Beware of a spiteful enemy who would like to take your wealth.
		Your dream is a troubling sign; you will soon receive some bad news.
		This dream predicts trouble with a waiter—be sure to tip well!
		Be careful and watchful in what you do; lately someone has been trying to stir up trouble in your life.
		Don't be overly trusting; this dream suggests someone close to you is not being honest.
		You will soon have a rather difficult time with a woman.
		Your dream predicts that your troubles will soon be over.
		Expect a gift of money, or a raise at work.
		Your dream foretells that you will go on a trip or leave your home within six months.

SIGN 1.	SIGN 2.	*LIBRA*
		Your dream indicates misfortune; be on your guard.
		Prepare for change; your dream predicts a journey or shift.
		A sad dream. It warns of a death in your family.
		Your dream predicts dating or marriage.
		If this was dreamed on a Tuesday, Wednesday, or Thursday night, it promises success to the dreamer.
		Your dream indicates loss; don't gamble as you will lose.
		Take care of your health! This dream warns of sickness.
		A lucky dream! Within six weeks of this dream fortune will smile upon you.
		Your dream predicts trouble for an absent friend; warn them!

SIGN 1.	SIGN 2.	*LIBRA*
		An excellent dream; your adversaries will fade away and you will have good luck.
		Your dream is of little importance; your life will be a mix of good and evil.
		Your dream is a fortunate one—your family will experience prosperity and find love.
		Illness near you has been prevented.
		Brace yourself for a hard month of struggle; but if you dreamed on a Sunday the omen is good.
		An unfortunate dream; worry, hard work, and stress are in your future.
		Your dream doesn't have much meaning.
		This dream foretells new friends and acquaintances.

HIEROGLYPHIC EMBLEM

VENUS

SIGN 1.	SIGN 2.	
		Your dream is very sad; you will experience deep sorrow and grief.
		Your dream signifies that your absent friends might need support. Give them a call!
		You will change your address or home in some way.
		An unfortunate dream; anxiety and trouble will surround you for a short while.
		Your dream is a fortunate one; expect joy and celebration.
		The dreamer will first experience disappointment, then will be rewarded with wealth.

SIGN 1.	SIGN 2.	*VENUS*
		If you dreamt it on the tenth day of the month or on Sunday, your dream foretells wealth in your middle age.
		Someone who you've been at odds with will soon leave your life.
		You'll soon see someone you've missed.
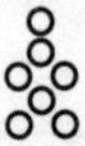		An unfortunate dream. Seven months of trouble are ahead.
		Your dream predicts anger, harsh words, and conflict; be careful.
		Beware of a dark-haired person in your life as they might cause you trouble.
		Fortune will smile on you; you've dreamed well.
		You will soon leave on a trip that will be prosperous.
		This dream signals love and marriage.

SIGN 1.	SIGN 2.	*VENUS*
		Beware of a redheaded man in your life.
		Be careful! Someone is talking about you behind your back.
		Your dream warns that you should not visit your rival.
		Your dream predicts that you will be worn down and tired, but will soon have easier days.
		You will soon hear of the death of someone you love who lives far away.
		Good fortune is on its way! Expect to receive a happy message or package.
		Your dream suggests that you will have a difficult season, but will overcome the obstacles you encounter.
		You will have disappointments at work or will receive a disappointing message.
		You will escape from a difficult situation unscathed.

SIGN 1.	SIGN 2.	*VENUS*
		Your work life will flourish and those you care about will enjoy love and happiness.
		This dream is good news for anyone in the public eye or for dreamers who travel frequently.
		Your dream foreshows difficulties, but they won't bother you too much.
		Don't be too trusting; friends are sometimes your biggest enemies.
		Don't travel for the next month.
		Your dream foretells sudden good luck.
		Someone is about to die.
		Take care of yourself; your health is in question.

HIEROGLYPHIC EMBLEM

SCORPIO

SIGN 1.	SIGN 2.	
o o o o o o	oo oo oo oo oo	Your dream is a fortunate one; your business will succeed beyond your expectations.
oo oo oo oo oo	o o o o o o	Your fate is about to change. Expect money, friends, prosperity, and happiness.
o o o o o	o oo oo oo oo	The dreamer will shortly take a trip that will turn out well.
o oo oo oo oo	o o o o o	An insignificant dream, it means little.
oo oo o o o	o o o oo oo oo	Hold off on making any big decisions; your fortune is about to improve.
o o o oo oo oo	oo oo o o o	You will learn the hard way that friends are fickle: a friend will prove to be a snake in the grass.

SIGN 1.	SIGN 2.	*SCORPIO*
		A victorious dream! Adversaries will oppose you, but you will win in the end.
		Take care of your health as sickness is around the corner.
		Expect news from distant friends, including one you haven't heard from in years.
		Your dream predicts a very profitable year.
		This dream warns you to be careful of lawyers and attorneys or you will lose money.
		Something you wish for will be granted to you.
		You will enjoy an unexpected monetary windfall, but be careful how you use it or you will lose it as suddenly as you receive it.
		You will receive a joyous surprise.
		Be careful who you trust and whose advice you take.

SIGN 1.	SIGN 2.	*SCORPIO*
		This is a dream of loss and grief.
		A happy dream! You'll be invited to a joyful celebration.
		If you're young this dream predicts love and marriage; if you're older it predicts contentment and peace.
		This dream suggests you have an admirer.
		An unfortunate dream. Be careful not to offend others.
		Be brave! You will overcome adversity.
		Beware! Gossip is being spread about you.
		Take care of your health; within three weeks you will get sick.
		Your dream foretells sadness and grief.

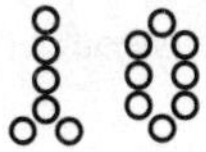

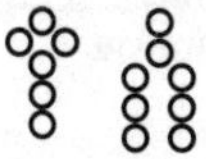

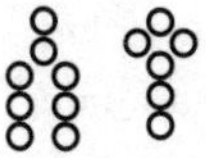

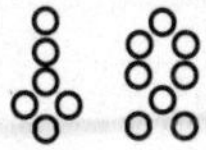

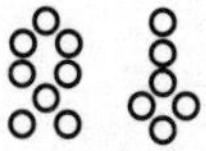

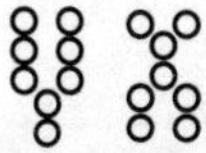

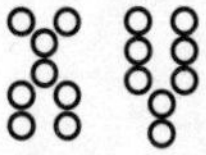

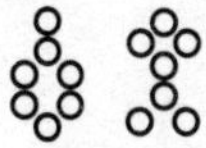

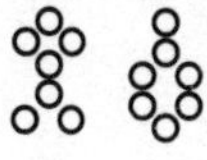

SIGN 1.	SIGN 2.	*SCORPIO*
		Your vision isn't important; nothing significant will happen to you.
		A quiet dream; your affairs will go on as usual.
		Your dream predicts a change in your fortune—travel, wealth, and happiness are in your future.
		Expect messages and mail, some of it including money, in the near future.
		You will have ill luck for a time.
		If dreamt on the fourth, fifth, or twentieth day of the month, your dream foretells a funeral.
		Your dream signifies fighting, anger, and strife.
		Your best friend will soon find themselves in trouble and need your help.

HIEROGLYPHIC EMBLEM

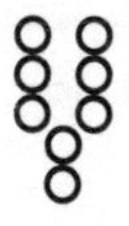

PALLAS

SIGN 1.	SIGN 2.	
		This dream doesn't bode well and will be worse at the new moon.
		Your dream warns you not to cross the ocean.
		Fortune is fickle as you will soon find out when you experience frustration and difficulties.
		Your dream foretells that much of your hard work will be in vain.
		A fortunate dream, signifying wealth and success in business and in love.
		Your dream promises happiness among family and friends.

SIGN 1.	SIGN 2.	*PALLAS*
		Beware of loss! Something will be stolen from you if you are not careful.
		Sorrow and sadness are in your future.
		Your dream is a very evil one; if you are in love you will experience loss; if you are in business you will suffer a setback.
		Your dream forecasts poor health ahead.
		Your dream predicts bad weather.
		This is a dream of hope, but don't be too optimistic.
		If dreamed on the first day of the month, your dream predicts a journey; on the third day, a friend; and deception and lies on any other day.
		You will be anxious and afraid, but don't worry as nothing bad will happen.

SIGN 1.	SIGN 2.	*PALLAS*
		You are about to go on a long trip that will prove beneficial.
		You will hear some alarming news that will upset you.
		A happy dream that tells of love, and joy, and celebration.
		This dream signifies that bad times are behind you.
		Beware of deception and double-dealing.
		Be careful who you trust; there are people who would injure you if they could.
		Your dream indicates new possibilities at work, a great deal of contemplation, and hard decisions.
		This is a dream of success in business and work.
		Your dream signifies the return of absent friends and traveling.

SIGN 1.	SIGN 2.	*PALLAS*
		This dream foretells that the nation will experience hardship.
		Beware of enemies and deceitful advisers; don't trust others.
		An unfavorable dream; disappointments and struggles in life and love.
		This dream foretells struggle in both love and business.
		Your dream predicts a loss of money or possession. Beware!
		Your fortune is about to change for the better, and you will soon receive money.
		Expect to hear good news within three days.
		Your dream signifies writing and books; there will be much studying and reading in your future.
		Be careful of the sea; this dream predicts danger.

HIEROGLYPHIC EMBLEM

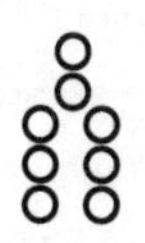

SAGITTARIUS

SIGN 1.	2.	
		Your dream is a good one; you will prosper.
		On a Saturday, this dream forebodes a restless mind; otherwise, it predicts money.
		Prepare for change and travel as your dream predicts that you'll go on a trip.
		You should prepare for change and restless times.
		A sad dream on the fifth, eighth, or twelfth day of the month, as it predicts funerals.
		Your dream is fortunate; it foreshadows good business and growth in your profit.

SIGN 1.	SIGN 2.	*SAGITTARIUS*
		An unfortunate dream for all things, as your vision indicates approaching grievances, trouble, and anxiety of mind.
		Sickness is about to enter your home. It will lay its hand on you, or on one whom you love.
		Your dream predicts that something is at risk.
		Your dream is a hard one and warns of loss and difficulty.
		Sadness and care are predicted by this dream; if you are in love your relationship will suffer.
		Your dream signifies traveling a long distance—either walking or in a vehicle.
		You can expect bad news that will cause you stress.
		Be careful! A friend you thought you knew will cause trouble for you.
		Your dream predicts that you will receive news from someone far away.

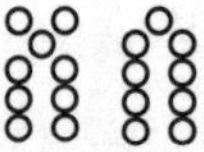

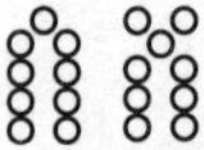

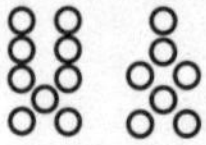

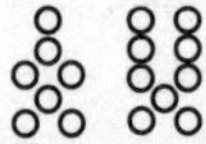

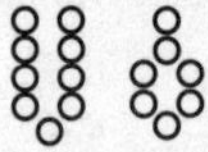

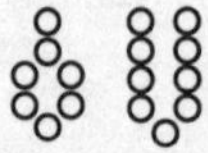

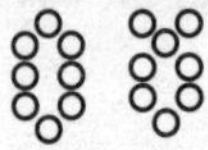

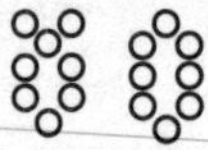

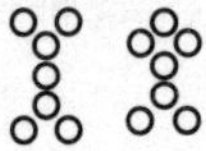

SIGN 1.	2.	*SAGITTARIUS*
		Something will happen soon that will prove frustrating.
		Your dream signifies happy times and a wedding in the family.
		Your dream foretells that your domestic life will be happy and content.
		Be careful you don't quarrel with anyone; your dream predicts anger.
		You will take a trip or a journey, or stop dreaming this dream.
		Your dream predicts that you will be injured if you approach a cow.
		You have a secret enemy near you—a tall, leonine person.
		Your dream promises good fortune.
		This dream signifies lawsuits, which you will do well to avoid.

SIGN 1.	SIGN 2.	*SAGITTARIUS*
O O O O O O O	O O O O O O O	Don't be discouraged; after some delays you will succeed.
O O O O O O O	O O O O O O O	This is a dream denoting money.
O O O O O O O	O O O O O O O	Your dream signifies danger during the current month. Beware and avoid water.
O O O O O O O	O O O O O O O	Your dream foretells festivities and celebrations.
O O O O O O O O	O O O O O O O O	This dream predicts sudden good fortune.
O O O O O O O O	O O O O O O O O	Be careful of theft; your dream suggests trouble with the law.
O O O O O O O O	O O O O O O O O	Your dream foretells some kind of disgrace. Take care!
O O O O O O O O	O O O O O O O O	This dream promises a happy life and good fortune.

HIEROGLYPHIC EMBLEM

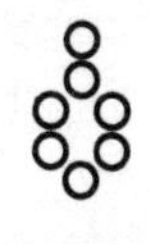

JUNO

SIGN

1.	2.	
		Your dream forebodes change for the worse, followed by possible improvement.
		You will soon hear of the loss of a friend.
		Your dream signifies the loss of a close friend within three months.
		Your dream prophesies that you will experience a costly move.
		Many things that you are undertaking will cause frustration.
		Your dream portends poor health.

SIGN 1.	SIGN 2.	*JUNO*
		This dream signifies too much small talk.
		Expect loss and disappointments; this is an unsettled time.
		Your dream is ominous of a loss by theft or cheating if dreamed on the ninth day of the month.
		Your dream signifies that an extraordinary accident will happen.
		This dream predicts either marriage or angry words.
		You can expect struggle in family life.
		After this dream you will gain the friendship of an older person.
		You have many envious detractors, but they won't be able to affect you.
		Your dream is unhappy; be careful!

SIGN 1.	2.	*JUNO*
		This dream signifies loss of wealth and misfortune.
		This dream is unreliable.
		Your dream signifies that gossip and lies are being told around you.
		You can expect to live to an old age and die content.
		Venus and Mercury bear lordship in your dream; your fortune is prosperous.
		Your dream speaks of prosperity, gain, and wealth.
		Beautiful women will cause trouble in your life.
		Be on your guard against backbiting friends.
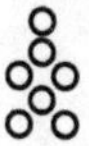		Avoid the water for some time after this dream.

SIGN 1.	SIGN 2.	*JUNO*
		Your dream is very evil; if dreamed on a Friday your expectations will be thwarted.
		Your dream predicts love letters in your future.
		This dream foretells pleasure after pain.
		You can expect to hear of the death of a neighbor.
		Your dream foretells poor health; take care!
		Sickness is in your future; be cautious!
		Your dream foretells mourning and conflict in your life.
		Many of your hopes will not come to be.

HIEROGLYPHIC EMBLEM

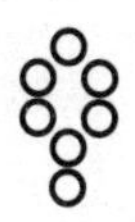

CAPRICORN

SIGN 1.	SIGN 2.	
		Your dream refers to faith or a religious friend that you will soon meet.
		Your dream foreshows trading, wealth, and counting money.
		To your surprise you will soon enjoy the friendship of powerful and influential people.
		You will soon receive a message and hear from a distant contact.
		Your dream suggests that liars and gossips are talking about you.
		Your dream predicts trouble and a period of unsettlement.

CAPRICORN

SIGN 1.	SIGN 2.	CAPRICORN
		You have had a vision of happiness—expect joy and prosperity.
		The dreamer may expect to hear some good news shortly.
		Dreamer, beware of too much pleasure; it will soon cause trouble.
		Your dream is under Venus, which foretells weddings or celebrations.
		Signs under Mars foretell of conflict and anger. Be careful!
		Beware of alarming surprises.
		Your dream forewarns you that thieves are nearby; proceed carefully.
		Your dream foretells good news.
		Expect sorrow and humiliation in the coming days.

SIGN 1.	SIGN 2.	*CAPRICORN*
		Your dream forebodes sadness and grief plaguing your mind.
		After all your troubles, you will now find safety and comfort.
		Your dream foretells the death of an enemy.
		You can expect to hear some good news soon.
		This is a vain dream; it is due to unresolved anger.
		Your dream foretells the departure of a strange guest and a message.
		This is a dream of lack and misfortune.
		This dream on a Friday means there will be news; Sunday, money; Monday, traveling; Tuesday, a quarrel; other days, strife.

SIGN 1.	SIGN 2.	*CAPRICORN*
		On a Thursday or Sunday your dream presages money; if on the twelfth day of the month, expect an inheritance.
		Your dream foretells advancement after hard work.
		Your dream prophesies the coming of a friend.
		This is a dream of lies and pointless words.
		You should be wary; adversity is nearby, though you will endure it.
		One who speaks poorly of you is nearby.
		Take care of your health; your dream predicts sickness.
		Your dream signifies bad news if dreamt on a Monday.
		Your dream indicates hard work with a small reward.

HIEROGLYPHIC EMBLEM

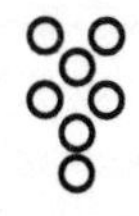

CERES

SIGN 1.	SIGN 2.	
		Dreamer, you are born to good fortune; even now the stars shine brightly on your horoscope.
		Your dream signals money and riches.
		You have a rival near at hand; your dream also signifies changes in business and work.
		Your vision is of little importance.
		Trouble is leaving you, and your fortune is changing for the better.
		Prepare for friends or a friend, as they'll soon arrive.

SIGN 1.	SIGN 2.	*CERES*
		A joyous dream! You will enjoy festivities and celebrations.
		Your dream, if on a Monday, predicts a marriage among friends; on other days, gladness.
		You will soon have news and letters from friends.
		Prepare for travel, as you will travel three times in the next year.
		Dreamer, your vision is a warning against false friends.
		You will lose a friend within the month.
		Beware of a spiteful competitor who is trying to hurt you.
		Your dream is evil, denoting some difficult months ahead.
		Prepare to lose money unless you are very mindful of your wallet.

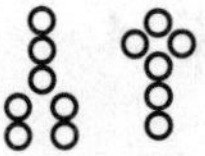

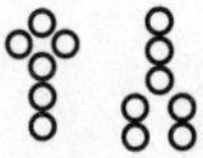

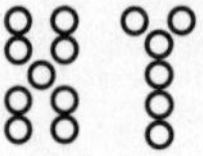

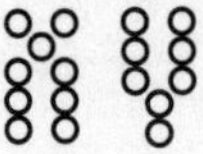

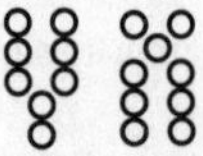

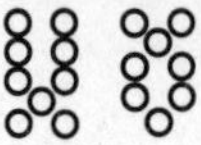

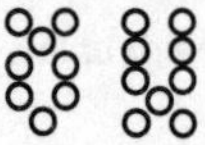

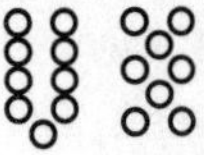

SIGN 1.	SIGN 2.	*CERES*
		Your dream implies that profit will come after loss in your life.
		A sorrow you have carried for some time will soon disappear.
		Your fears will vanish soon.
		Your dream warns you to be careful, as there is a risk you will fall and injure yourself.
		Great sorrow will come in the year after this dream; you will lose a relative.
		Your dream predicts a funeral.
		Your vision foretells the loss of a friend who is abroad.
		Thieves are nearby; be careful of your home.
		Your dream foretells loss if dreamed on the second, fourth, or other even days of the month; on other days, it means difficulty is coming.

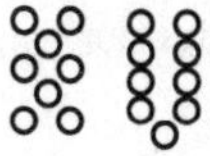

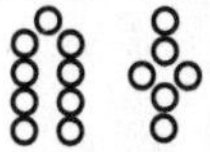

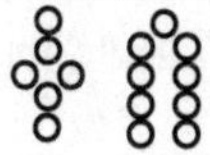

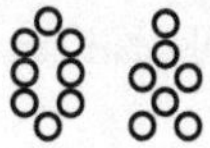

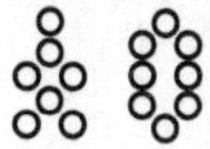

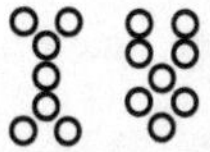

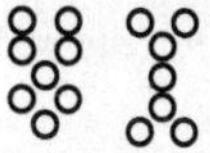

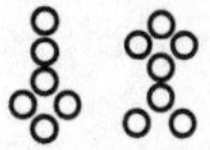

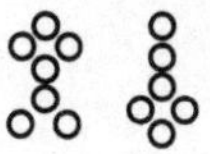

CERES

SIGN 1.	SIGN 2.	
		Your dream indicates that a spiteful adversary will disappear from your life.
		This dream represents tears—trouble is nearby.
		A good dream, if dreamt on a Thursday, foretelling a happy year to follow.
		This dream predicts a mix of happiness and sadness in your future.
		Your dream predicts heavy burdens in your life.
		This is a good dream only on a Saturday; on other days it predicts misfortune.
		Your dream is good; you can expect to receive a large sum of money.
		You have dreamed well; peace and prosperity are in your future.

HIEROGLYPHIC EMBLEM

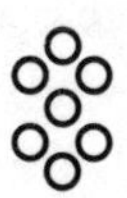

AQUARIUS

SIGN 1.	2.	
○ ○ ○ ○ ○ ○ ○	○ ○ ○ ○ ○ ○ ○ ○ ○ ○	Dreamer, you have been warned of great disappointment in your future.
○ ○ ○ ○ ○ ○ ○ ○ ○ ○	○ ○ ○ ○ ○ ○ ○	After this dream, avoid going near the water.
○ ○ ○ ○ ○	○ ○ ○ ○ ○ ○ ○ ○	You will be disappointed in money; be mindful of your wallet.
○ ○ ○ ○ ○ ○ ○ ○	○ ○ ○ ○ ○	Your dream is a fortunate one.
○ ○ ○ ○ ○ ○ ○	○ ○ ○ ○ ○ ○ ○ ○	Your dream warns against people who will lie about you.
○ ○ ○ ○ ○ ○ ○ ○	○ ○ ○ ○ ○ ○ ○	Your dream signifies that some of your family, or very close neighbors, do not have your best interests at heart.

SIGN 1.	SIGN 2.	*AQUARIUS*
		On the ninth or thirteenth day of the month this dream means that trusted counselors in your life have deceived you.
		Be careful of false friends who do not support you.
		Your dream indicates much activity and busyness, perhaps involving travel.
		Your dream predicts anxiety and trouble; you can expect an unsettled time.
		An unfortunate dream; it forebodes many gloomy prospects for the dreamer.
		You will soon hear news of a friend who is in severe trouble; and if dreamt on a Thursday, it foretells a funeral.
		Your dream is under the star of Venus, so you have dreamed well. Expect good fortune.
		A woman will lead to loss in your life, but friendship will follow.

SIGN 1.	SIGN 2.	*AQUARIUS*
		Beware, dreamer, of someone close to you who will prove deceitful.
		Your dream indicates fear of sickness and ill health.
		You will soon become acquainted with a person who will prove a faithful and trustworthy friend.
		Prepare for travel and a change of address.
		You will have news of absent friends, and will receive messages or letters.
		Your dream suggests that you have a powerful rival.
		You have had an unfortunate dream; sickness is nearby.
		You will be rescued from your troubles, but not before they prove irritating.
		You will soon receive some money.

AQUARIUS

SIGN 1.	SIGN 2.	
		Your dream was more enjoyable than it was fortunate.
		Your dream indicates several things: first, it foretells a theft in your life, then a present, and, finally, a funeral.
		Fortune will trouble your wallet, health, and property.
		On a Monday your dream shows trouble; the same on a Wednesday; but on other days it indicates news.
		You will shortly hear news of absent friends.
		Take care of yourself! After your dream it will be difficult to escape danger.
		Be careful of four-footed animals, as your dream predicts you will be injured by one.
		This dream foretells the loss of some goods or possessions.
		Your dream suggests that you will be poor in your youth, but wealthy in old age.

HIEROGLYPHIC EMBLEM

VESTA

SIGN 1.	SIGN 2.	
		Dreamer, you are lucky! Friends and money will appear in your life and you will enjoy this dream three times in seven years.
		Your dream signifies you will benefit from the death of someone in a foreign country.
		Your vision is of little or no importance.
		Prepare for travel; your dream signifies change.
		Your dream predicts that you will shortly receive an inheritance.
		An excellent dream; the stars of heaven smile upon you and you will experience a run of good luck.

SIGN 1.	SIGN 2.	*VESTA*
		You can expect to be invited to a wedding.
		Your dream predicts a wedding in the family.
		You can expect a lot of news in the coming month; some of it will be bad news about a friend.
		You have a secret rival and you will soon learn their identity.
		Your dream is a warning to be careful; an accident may happen near your home.
		Keep an eye on those around you; there is a risk of fraud and deception.
		Your dream entails struggle and hard days ahead.
		Your dream is one of fortune and prosperity; wealth will come in many unexpected ways.
		Oh, dreamer! Look around you; there are many who would speak badly of you.

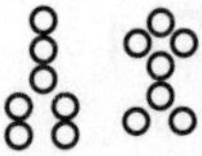

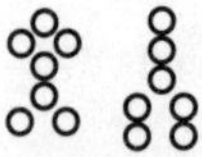

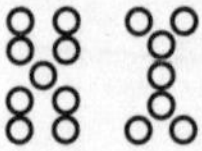

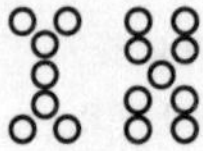

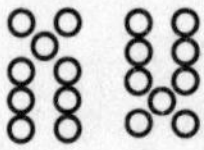

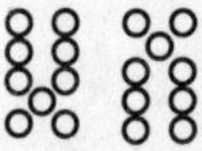

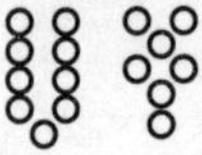

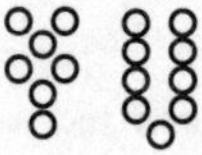

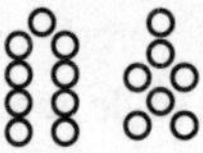

SIGN 1.	SIGN 2.	*VESTA*
		Your dream is conflicted; good things will be brought about by something bad.
		Some of your friends are in serious trouble.
		Your dream signifies anger and conflict.
		Marriage or friendship is predicted by this dream.
		Dreamer, be careful what you drink; this dream hints at a danger of poison.
		Trials and losses are about to enter your life.
		Your dream has no particular significance; it was simply the wandering of your mind.
		Your dream foretells the coming of ambition, advancement, and growth.
		Your vision suggests that a religious person will become a good friend to you.

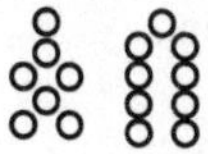

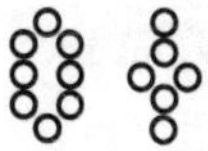

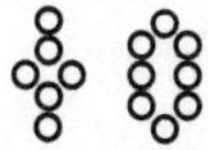

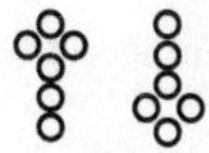

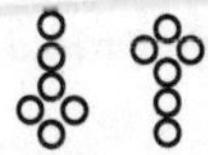

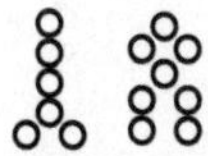

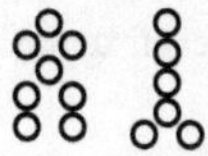

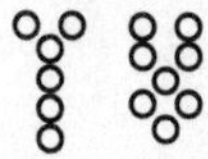

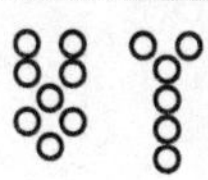

SIGN 1.	SIGN 2.	*VESTA*
		Your wishes will not be fulfilled.
		After this vision you can expect sorrow and grief.
		You will soon be saved from a danger that you frequently fall into.
		A joyous and fortunate dream; good will soon follow the hard times you've experienced.
		Your dream indicates that you are a faithful friend, but that many of your friends are not.
		Be careful of falling objects!
		You have many enemies, but you will prevail against them.
		Your dream means long life, but much of it will be spent in sorrow.

HIEROGLYPHIC EMBLEM

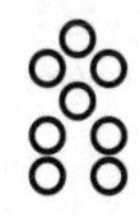

PISCES

SIGN 1.	2.	
o o o o o o o o	o o o o o o o o o o	Prepare for hard days and to lose money.
o o o o o o o o o o	o o o o o o o o	You will be disappointed in your business and personal affairs.
o o o o o	o o o o o o o	Your dream predicts a great deal of traveling and walking, along with many changes in your life.
o o o o o o o	o o o o o	Tidy up the house! A friend is coming over soon.
o o o o o o o	o o o o o o o	Your dream has to do with gold and silver.
o o o o o o o	o o o o o o o	After this dream, you will have trouble with money.

SIGN 1.	SIGN 2.	*PISCES*
		Be careful of deceitful people who are working against your interests.
		Your dream forewarns that if you lend money you will lose it.
		Shortly after this dream you will receive a hasty message or letter.
		Your dream promises a busy social life and many friends.
		Your dream doesn't have any particular meaning.
		Watch your step! Your dream predicts an accident or fall.
		Your dream is warning of coming danger; don't travel for a month afterward.
		This dream predicts either a relationship or a rival.
		If your dream was on the eleventh day of the month, it foreshows frustration; otherwise it means change is coming.

SIGN 1.	SIGN 2.	*PISCES*
		Messages or news will reach your ears that will cause frustration.
		Your dream is joyful and indicates celebrations in your future.
		Get ready for a party; your dream predicts a wedding in your family.
		You are about to undergo a dramatic change for the better; your work will benefit from it.
		Your dream foretells that you will soon receive a large sum of money.
		This is an unfortunate dream, denoting strife, conflict, and fear.
		Your dream is full of deceitfulness and uselessness.
		Dreamer, you have had a strange dream; you will lose someone within a year.
		Your dream warns against the threat of fire—be careful!

PISCES

SIGN 1.	SIGN 2.	
		Your dream predicts that news and messages are coming to you.
		Things that are frustrating you now will soon no longer be a problem.
		Strangers or friends are about to pay you a visit; prepare for them!
		Your dream foretells traveling.
		You must be careful of false friends.
		Your dream is fortunate—joy, love, and prosperity.
		You have had a bad dream; on the third or seventh day of the month, it indicates sickness; on other days, struggle and sadness.
		Your dream signifies frustration, grief, and trouble.

HIEROGLYPHIC EMBLEM

DIANA

SIGN 1.	2.	
		Good fortune is coming.
		Busyness and activity are predicted; your work will pay off.
		Your dream predicts that secrets will be revealed.
		Avoid the water; it would be dangerous for you.
		Your dream is a happy one; it foretells a time of prosperity.
		The stars are shining kindly on you. Your dream speaks of money and possessions in the coming season.

SIGN 1.	SIGN 2.	*DIANA*
		Your dream is an unfortunate one; many events will occur but the outcome will not be positive.
		An evil dream, denoting sadness and loss in business.
		You will be involved in something relating to criminal activity.
		Prepare for a season of ill health.
		Your dream signifies you must be careful of secret adversaries who are working against you.
		Your dream forewarns of some confusion relating to documents and legal matters; be careful what you sign.
		You had a pleasant and profitable dream that suggests business will be good.
		Expect to hear some good news soon.
		During the waxing moon, your dream foretells disasters; during the waning moon, it predicts loss.

SIGN 1.	SIGN 2.	*DIANA*
		Your dream predicts that you should prepare for bad news that will be distressing.
		A fortunate dream; you will have a long life with wealth, honor, and good fortune.
		This dream brings happiness and contentment.
		This dream predicts marriage or children.
		A sad dream, predicting tears and heartbreak.
		Your dream foretells anger and fighting.
		A doubtful dream. Be careful.
		You can disregard this dream.
		Your vision is dark, obscure, and does not have any clear portents.

SIGN 1.	SIGN 2.	*DIANA*
		You have had a dream that tells of fellowship and happiness.
		Your dream indicates that you will soon lose money.
		Your dream is one of misfortune and difficulty.
		Your dream is fortunate if dreamt on the first, fifth, or eleventh day of the month; on other days, it is a warning of evil.
		Hard times will follow after this dream.
		This dream foretells temptations and trials.
		Your dream warns you to remember that a duplicitous friend is near you.
		You will be frustrated by books and writing.

HIEROGLYPHIC EMBLEM

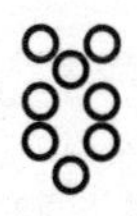

MEDUSA

SIGN 1.	2.	
		Dreamer, beware of a redheaded person.
		If you are wealthy this dream is a sign of trouble to come; if you are not then it predicts a rise in your fortune.
		Be careful of your actions; this dream threatens shame and reproach.
		Sickness is about to visit your home.
		If you are poor, this dream indicates that you will become wealthy; if not it warns you to be careful.
		This dream indicates an amorous friendship.

SIGN 1.	SIGN 2.	*MEDUSA*
		You will lose a reliable coworker or employee.
		Protect your home; this dream warns of a thief.
		If you had this dream on a Thursday, it is a sure omen of many happy years to come, but it is also a good dream on any other day.
		Your dream indicates that you are about to receive some strange and hasty news.
		Take care of yourself; your dream is a sign of an accident to come.
		This dream threatens danger.
		Your dream indicates that you will soon experience grief.
		Your dream is a fortunate one; you can expect a promotion.
		Your dream predicts that you will endure some trouble, but will receive money.

SIGN 1.	SIGN 2.	*MEDUSA*
		This dream foretells the loss or damage of your property.
		This dream warns against a serious mishap that will happen in the next three months; be careful.
		If you had this dream on the seventh day of the month, it is a sign that you will lose large sums of money.
		There will be both a wedding and a funeral within the next twelve months.
		You have many rivals; be cautious.
		Your dream indicates that you will enjoy pleasure, but it will be deceptive.
		You will travel and work, but your goal will remain elusive.
		You will experience frustration due to your adversaries, but in the end you will be victorious.

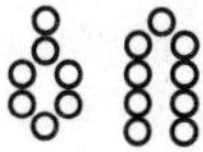

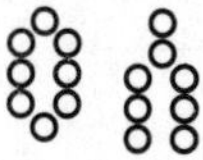

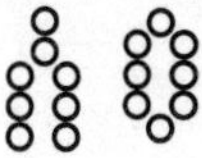

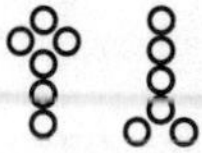

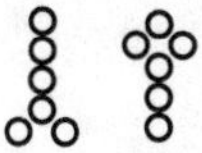

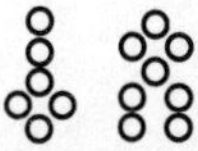

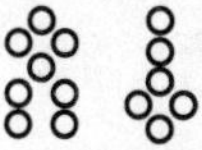

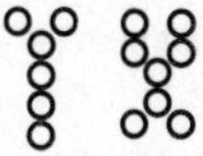

SIGN 1.	SIGN 2.	*MEDUSA*
		Your dream means: on Tuesday, money; on Wednesday or Friday, gifts; on Monday, a friend; on Thursday, a ring: on Saturday, a rival; on Sunday, a journey.
		Your dream foretells money.
		Your dream predicts good fortune; you will be happy and wealthy in your old age.
		Keep an eye on your wallet! Your dream suggests that you will lose money unexpectedly.
		Your dream foretells hardship and difficulty.
		Your dream does not bring good things.
		Your dream foretells a snag in your plans.
		Your dream predicts grief and sadness of heart and mind.
		The dream foretells sudden anger.

HIEROGLYPHIC EMBLEM

PHOEBUS

SIGN 1.	2.	
		Your dream signifies sadness, grief, and sorrow.
		Be careful and avoid going near the water.
		Your dream foretells theft or a secret rival. Be on your guard!
		You are about to hear some very good news.
		This dream predicts marriage and happiness.
		This dream predicts wellness for those who are sick, but for others it is unprofitable.

SIGN 1.	SIGN 2.	*PHOEBUS*
		Your dream promises profit and gain; your business will do well.
		Your dream foretells deliverance from all your troubles.
		If dreamt on a Wednesday this dream foretells marriage; on a Sunday, gain; and on any other day it promises good friends.
		Your dream predicts that you will receive a reward.
		To the wealthy, your dream indicates secret envy, but to the poor it signifies financial relief.
		If you are not mindful of this dream, grief and trouble will surround you.
		On the thirteenth day of the month your dream foretells death; on any other day it shows that illness is coming.
		A new endeavor will prove successful after this dream.

SIGN 1.	SIGN 2.	*PHOEBUS*
		You will discover hidden secrets.
		Your dream predicts that an adversary or rival will fail in their goals.
		A very fortunate dream; you are fated to become rich and respected.
		You are about to be invited to a party or celebration.
		Death will take one of your rivals.
		You will soon be invited to a wedding or celebration.
		Your dream warns of spiteful rivals.
		Your dream predicts a funeral.
		Your dream foretells that you will become acquainted with new friends, but be cautious of them.

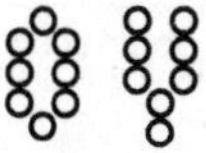

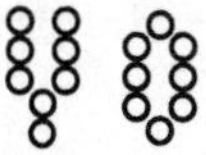

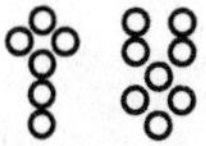

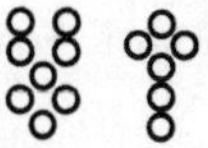

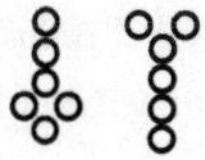

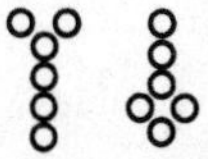

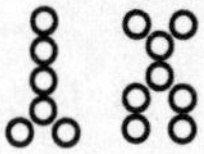

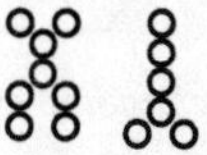

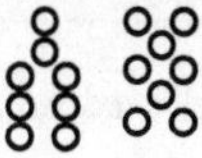

SIGN 1.	SIGN 2.	*PHOEBUS*
		This dream promises that you will soon receive money.
		Your wishes will soon be fulfilled.
		Your dream warns of sad news.
		This dream signifies an obstacle or delay in your work.
		On a Sunday this dream foretells love; on Monday, sickness; on Wednesday, a gift; on Friday, friendship; any other days it predicts loss.
		Be careful what you write; it will cause trouble.
		You have many personal rivals; they will create obstacles for you.
		Be careful of a tall, fair man. He will become an adversary.
		This dream predicts that you will be released from some fear or pain that has been looming over you.

HIEROGLYPHIC EMBLEM

HECATE

SIGN 1.	SIGN 2.	
o o o o o o o	o o o o o o o o o o	Your dream is a fortunate one; it predicts happiness and good business prospects.
o o o o o o o o o o	o o o o o o o	Your dream predicts happiness, celebration, singing, and joy.
o o o o o	o o o o o o o o	Your dream foretells sadness, but it will be followed by joy.
o o o o o o o o	o o o o o	Your dream forewarns you of many competitive rivals and adversaries.
o o o o o o o	o o o o o o o o	Your dream signifies that a wealthy person will become your friend and partner.
o o o o o o o o	o o o o o o o	This dream predicts a delay at work.

SIGN 1.	SIGN 2.	*HECATE*
		Your dream promises that you will receive money.
		Your vision symbolizes great success and happiness in your life.
		You will soon hear some very bad news.
		Someone near you is gossiping behind your back; be cautious.
		On any day except the third day of the month this is an unlucky dream.
		This dream on a Tuesday predicts a rival; on a Monday, a friend, but a deceitful one; on all other days it is unimportant.
		Your dream predicts happiness and good company.
		There will be celebration and festivities, but they will end poorly for you.
		You will be invited to a wedding.

SIGN 1.	SIGN 2.	*HECATE*
		Your dream signifies that before long you will lose a friend you respected deeply.
		You will be invited to a party.
		You will find success in your endeavors.
		Your dream foretells that you will soon move or find a new home.
		You are about to receive some urgent and very strange news.
		This dream foretells profit in your work and a season of busyness.
		You will make a close friend soon.
		Your dream was pleasant and profitable.
		You can expect sickness to visit your home.

SIGN 1.	SIGN 2.	*HECATE*
		Your dream forewarns of disaster if you dreamt it on a Friday; otherwise it foretells sadness.
		Your dream warns against a false friend.
		Your dream predicts that something you have long wished for will be delayed.
		Messages and news are coming your way.
		A spiteful person is envious of you.
		Your dream foretells death in your family.
		Your dream signifies that you will travel soon.
		You should behave discreetly; there are many eyes on you.

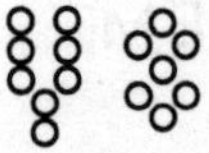

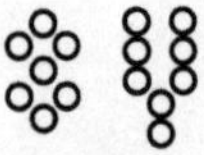

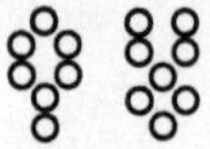

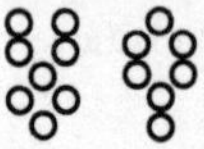

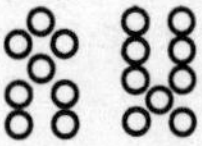

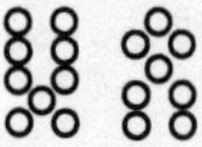

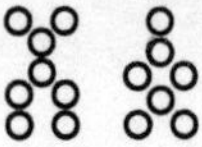

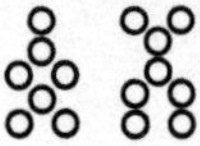

HIEROGLYPHIC EMBLEM

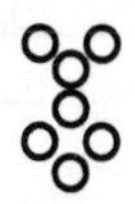

APOLLO

SIGN 1.	2.	
		Your dream predicts future honor and dignity.
		You are about to receive some money.
		Your dream is an unprofitable one.
		Your dream warns of trouble from a variety of sources.
		This dream is a sign of joy and happiness.
		You will be blessed with health, wealth, and friends.

SIGN 1.	SIGN 2.	*APOLLO*
		Your dream indicates success at work and in business.
		Your dream warns that something evil is nearby.
		Conflict with rivals is coming your way.
		Your dream symbolizes deception, but if you are careful you can escape untouched.
		This dream forewarns against a coming misfortune.
		On a Sunday your dream predicts evil; on a Monday, news; on a Tuesday, treachery; on a Wednesday, messages; other days, anger.
		Your dream is remarkably good; it foretells years of abundance and happiness.
		If you're married, expect fighting; if you're dating, prepare for a rival.
		Your dream forewarns that you will soon lose one of your family or friends.

SIGN 1.	SIGN 2.	*APOLLO*
		Your dream signifies many adversaries.
		This dream is good; it foretells money and wealth.
		Your dream signifies anger about money.
		You will receive a promotion.
		Your dream predicts that you will receive bad news, but nothing will harm you.
		A funeral is looming.
		Your dream warns of sickness and poor health.
		If dreamt on the third, fifth, seventh, or tenth days of the month, this dream is a sure sign of a death within the year.
		Your dream is merely a product of an anxious mind and is not prophetic.

SIGN 1.	SIGN 2.	*APOLLO*
		This dream means bad fortune.
		You have many secret rivals so be on your guard.
		On a Sunday this dream means you will receive a present; on a Thursday, loss through a bad debt; on other days, it is not significant.
		Your dream predicts that many troubles lie before you.
		This dream is good and signifies money.
		Your dream indicates small pleasures.
		You will soon meet kind friends.
		Your dream indicates happiness, new experiences, and a joyful time.

HIEROGLYPHIC EMBLEM

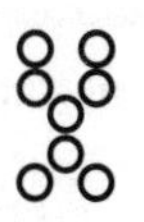

FORTUNE

SIGN 1.	SIGN 2.	
		Your dream warns of a funeral within the year.
		Your dream predicts unhappiness.
		Your dream will cause you to be unlucky for a season.
		On a Saturday this dream predicts an accident; on any other day, trouble.
		You are about to be blessed with luck and good fortune.
		After a season of spending, this dream foretells of prosperity.

SIGN 1.	SIGN 2.	*FORTUNE*
		Your dream forewarns you to be careful who you trust.
		This dream predicts trouble from a man.
		You can expect to hear some unexpected news.
		Your dream predicts a great deal of business and activity.
		Be aware of a false friend who is not what they seem to be.
		Don't lend your money or you will lose it.
		Your dream signifies that something joyful is coming your way.
		Your dream predicts happiness and contentment.
		This dream warns you that a friend is ill.

SIGN 1.	SIGN 2.	*FORTUNE*
		Dreamer, be careful who you speak against.
		If you are not careful, anger will get the best of you.
		Something will be removed or lost from your life.
		This dream foretells disappointment.
		Your dream warns of secret adversaries.
		This dream signifies that something unpleasant is about to happen in your home or near you.
		There is a hidden rival in your life; be careful.
		If you dreamed on a Sunday, your dream shows a sudden piece of good news; Monday, a quarrel; other days, that money is coming.
		This dream is an omen of great prosperity.

SIGN 1.	SIGN 2.	*FORTUNE*
		You will soon encounter someone who is trying to help you.
		If you are single this dream predicts marriage or partnership.
		Your dream is fortunate, and your wishes will be fulfilled.
		This dream predicts money and friends.
		Your dream foretells a series of delays, followed by prosperity.
		You are in danger from an animal; be careful.
		Something you wish for will be delayed.
		You have had an unfortunate dream.

HIEROGLYPHIC EMBLEM

NEPTUNE

SIGN 1.	SIGN 2.	
		On the second day of the month, this dream signifies you will receive wealth; on other days, travel and news.
		Your dream signifies that you can expect an increase in your business.
		This is an unfortunate dream.
		You can expect some unhappiness after this dream.
		Your dream is prosperous and good; it also promises a promotion.
		Your dream signifies that you will achieve wealth and power.

SIGN 1.	SIGN 2.	*NEPTUNE*
		This vision promises prosperity and marriage.
		You have many rivals, but this dream signifies that you will outdo them.
		You can expect to be annoyed and insulted by some of your enemies.
		Your dream warns you to be careful of being involved with the law.
		Look after your health; this dream is a sign of sickness.
		Your dream signifies trouble and sadness within a year.
		Your dream foretells bad news.
		Your dream predicts success and comfort for your whole life.
		To the sick this dream promises a speedy recovery.

SIGN 1. 2.	*NEPTUNE*
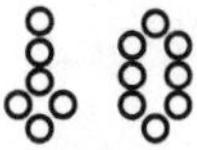	The day after this dream you should not undertake any big business decisions.
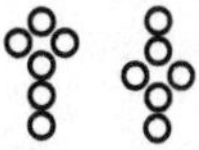	This dream predicts a happy relationship with someone you love.
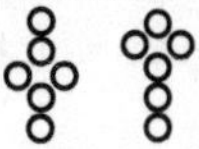	You will be invited to a special gathering.
	After this dream you will experience trouble.
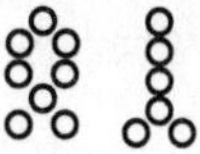	Your dream signifies that you have adversaries who will frustrate you greatly.
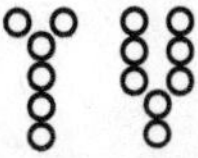	If dreamt on Wednesday, Thursday, or Friday your dream predicts that you will gain wealth; on other days, friends.
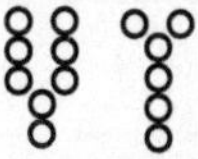	Your dream is fortunate and prosperity will mark your path.
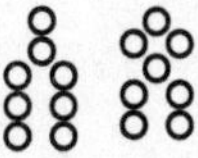	This dream signifies prosperity in business and work.
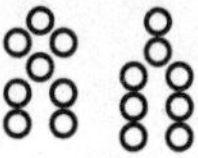	Your dream predicts that things will fall into line and you will have peace of mind soon.

SIGN 1.	SIGN 2.	*NEPTUNE*
		Your dream signifies pain, hard work, and grief.
		Beware! Adversaries are working against you.
		You have had a fortunate dream; it predicts wealth in your future.
		Your dream is about friends; prepare your home for absent friends will come to see you.
		You will experience trouble in your relationships.
		This dream signifies marriage.
		A person you have long believed to be a friend will become a rival.
		Your dream signifies that bad news is nearby.

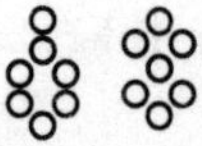

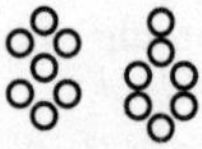

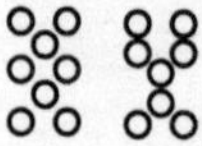

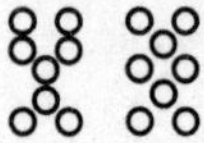

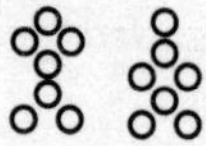

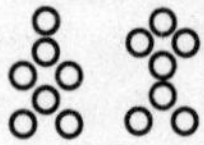

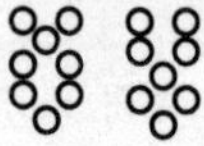

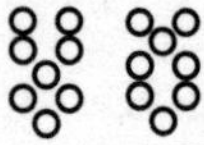

HIEROGLYPHIC EMBLEM

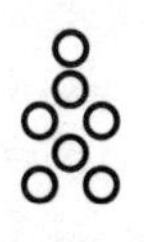

ORION

SIGN 1.	SIGN 2.	
		Your dream predicts your business will not succeed and things will go wrong.
		This vision has an evil interpretation.
		Your dream signifies that many things will not go as you hope.
		Your dream is very fortunate; you will escape from serious trouble with the help of a friend.
		You will soon receive help from a person who is higher up than yourself.
		You should be careful of four-footed animals.

SIGN 1.	SIGN 2.	*ORION*
		Sickness is coming; be careful of your health.
		On a Sunday, Tuesday, or Thursday, your dream signifies honor and respect; on other days, friendship.
		This dream predicts that a vile person will speak poorly of you; be careful.
		This dream forewarns of sadness and anxiety.
		Your dream is of little importance on the sixth, seventh, or ninth days of the month; other days, it warns of sickness in your family.
		Your dream is unfortunate, indicating a loss of reputation and friendship.
		An unfortunate dream: your destiny will be hard to achieve.
		You must beware of overeating and drinking too much; it will result in sickness and trouble.
		This dream precedes good fortune and happiness.

SIGN 1.	SIGN 2.	*ORION*
		The signs foretell anger and conflict.
		Your dream is a good sign; it indicates a long, happy life and good fortune.
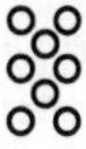		Your dream predicts money and riches in good time.
		This dream forebodes an obstacle in your path.
		You will soon learn of an inheritance.
		Your dream promised many things, but they are all illusions, and will come to nothing.
		Be on your guard. Many slippery friends are around you; be careful what you say and do.
	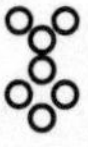	You will soon go on a long trip.
		Your dream predicts that by your wit and skill you will earn a lot of money.

SIGN 1.	SIGN 2.	*ORION*
		If dreamt on a Saturday, expect an expensive present; on a Sunday, a journey; on a Wednesday, hard work without reward; other days, profit.
		Your dream predicts a wedding if dreamt during a waxing moon.
		Your dream signifies news, messages, and updates.
		You must be cautious of troublesome, petty people or you will regret it.
		Pay attention to those around you; someone may be gossiping.
		This dream implies strife and conflict.
		Your dream forewarns that misfortune is approaching; you will lose money.
		Be careful and many of your current troubles will disappear.

HIEROGLYPHIC EMBLEM

FINIS

SIGN 1.	SIGN 2.	
		A difficult person who causes trouble is nearby. Be careful.
		Your dream is a sign of anger and conflict. Be careful to avoid drama.
		Your dream predicts good things for your work and business.
		Your dream speaks of flitting from place to place, change, and travel.
		Your dream foretells that you will escape from bad luck and be successful.
		Your dream foretells that you will thrive and succeed where you are.

SIGN 1.	SIGN 2.	*FINIS*
		You must be careful; you are likely to be wronged by friends or neighbors.
		Your dream indicates brisk business.
		Be careful of advisers who are more optimistic than they are honest.
		Your dream is a hard one—it foretells hard work and much labor.
		Your dream was the result of an unsettled mind.
		You will make a powerful friend.
		Your dream signifies marriage, but be careful of marrying too quickly.
		A proud person is envious of you.
		Your dream is good, and predicts wealth in your old age.

SIGN 1.	SIGN 2.	*FINIS*
		You have rivals, but you will overcome them.
		Be careful! You have many detractors and false friends.
		Your dream warns that you have hidden rivals, but you will overcome them.
		Do not risk going near water; it is dangerous right now.
		Your dream warns of a coming funeral.
		A person you have befriended will frustrate you and be ungrateful.
		Your vision is one of trouble and change.
		Your dream warns that you have a secret adversary.
		If dreamt on a Tuesday, your dream foretells victory; otherwise it is bad.

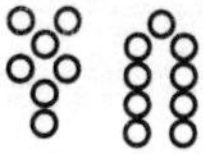

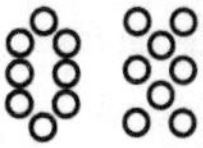

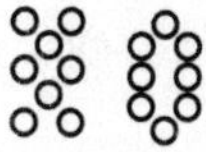

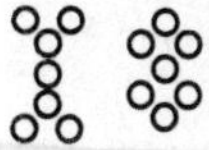

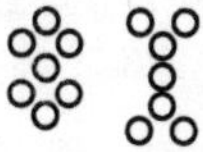

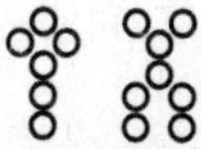

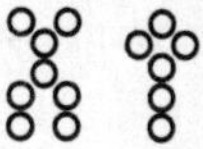

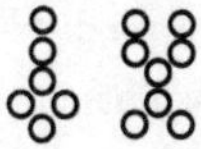

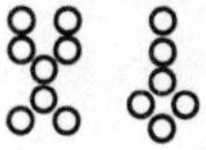

SIGN 1.	SIGN 2.	*FINIS*
		Misfortune will surround you.
		Your dream predicts trouble, but it will not last.
		Your dream foretells good fortune and success.
		This dream is a sign of a coming engagement.
		This dream foretells difficulty in love.
		Your dream was disturbing, but no harm will come to you.
		You should not put too much confidence in friends.
		On a Tuesday or Saturday your dream predicts a quarrel; on a Friday, a new relationship; other days, nothing of importance.

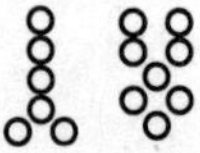

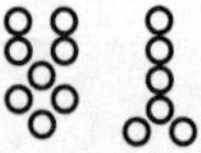

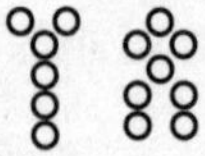

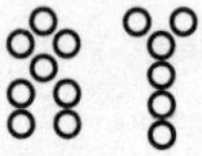

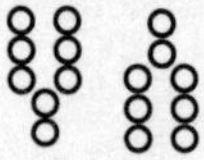

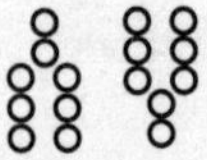

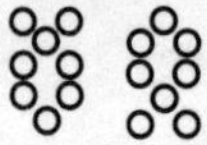

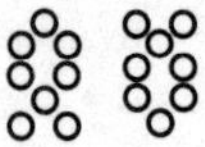

ABOUT THE AUTHORS

Several people wrote using the pseudonym Raphael, in reference to the biblical angel, during the nineteenth century. The Raphael responsible for *The Dream Book* is perhaps Robert Thomas Cross, who took up the pseudonym when he began editing *The Prophetic Messenger*, an astrological almanac. He was a prolific writer on a variety of subjects and was well known during his time for making astrology more accessible.

Dr. Michael Lennox is a spiritual teacher, psychologist, astrologer, and expert on dreams. Author of several books, including *Dream Sight* and *Llewellyn's Complete Dictionary of Dreams*, he conducts a worldwide practice of counseling and teaching from his home in Southern California.